JAMES MARTIN

Slow COOKING

MOUTHWATERING RECIPES WITH MINIMUM EFFORT

PHOTOGRAPHY BY TARA FISHER

Quadrille
PUBLISHING

Publishing director: Jane O'Shea
Creative director: Helen Lewis
Project editor: Laura Gladwin
Art direction & design: Gabriella Le Grazie
Photographer: Tara Fisher
Food stylists: Chris Start & Janet Brinkworth
Props stylist: Liz Belton
Production: Aysun Hughes

First published in 2012 by
Quadrille Publishing Limited
Alhambra House, 27–31 Charing Cross Road,
London WC2H 0LS
www.quadrille.co.uk

Cataloguing in Publication Data: a catalogue record
for this book is available from the British Library.

978 184949 123 5

Printed in China

cooking slow

Remember the food your grandmother used to make? The cakes, stews and casseroles filling the house with the most memorable smells? Even before the lid was removed, or the oven door was opened, you just knew it was going to be good because of the delicious aroma. It's the smell that makes it worth waiting for. When it comes to slow cooking, you know what I'm talking about!

Slow cooking is the ultimate in foolproof, stress-free food. It's all about minimum effort and maximum flavour, mainly because it usually involves using cuts of meat and vegetables that aren't too expensive. My family were pig and cattle farmers, so we used to eat the best food there was. My mother would put a beef stew in the slow cooker before we left for school, and it would tick over for eight hours, slowly bubbling while I was at school learning all about the genetic make-up of eggs. All she did at the end was to add the suet dumplings while we mucked out the pigs, and then it was ready. The stew filled the whole farmhouse with smells better than those of any Michelin-starred meal I've eaten. It was there that I learnt the art of slow cooking. My mum had learnt it from my gran, my gran from her mum, and so on. It just made perfect sense to them to use cheaper cuts of meat, and to cook them well.

Of course, all of this was before chefs came along with their fancy test-tube cooking and unachievable recipes that need endless equipment, a science lab and 12 people to help prepare them! That's not real cooking as far as I'm concerned. Cooking is a science, of course, but it's a simple application of heat to good-quality ingredients. Most of us would choose a beef stew and steamed sponge pudding over a picture on a plate. In fact, ask any chef what their favourite meal is and it will almost certainly be the last good meal they had at home. I learnt the art of cooking by coming to London and then travelling around Europe working in restaurants, but it's the slow-cooked dishes I remember the most. I learnt to make the best confit of duck from a French grandmother in Bordeaux when I was 13; I remember cooking braised lamb shanks with beans, tomatoes and olive oil mash at age 17; and, later, slowly cooking pigs' trotters in a three Michelin-starred restaurant in the heart of London. It's these dishes I remember more than any others, so I jumped at the chance to write my first book on slow cooking.

There are a few key things to be aware of when cooking slowly. Firstly, it's all about the ingredients. Being a Yorkshire man and having been brought up on a farm, I've learnt to keep things as simple as possible. It helps to understand that whatever part of the animal does the most work needs the longest cooking, but has the best flavour. So look out for lamb neck, trotters and shoulder of pork next time you're buying meat: they're such cheap cuts to buy, and any butcher will be only too glad to sell them to you. Thankfully, many chefs are coming round to this way of thinking, too, and pigs' cheeks and pork belly are staples on many restaurant menus these days. We should follow their lead, as the ingredients available have never been as good as they are nowadays, with artisan producers selling excellent quality produce all over the country.

I'm hoping this book inspires you to dig out that old casserole dish or slow cooker in the back of the cupboard. Dust it off and have a go! You don't need any new gadgets for these recipes – many of them can be done in a slow cooker or pressure cooker if you have one, but they're not essential. I was brought up with slow cookers, and thankfully they're coming back to the shop shelves. They're great to cook with, and you can do more with them than you might think. The best recipes to cook in them are the ones where the meat doesn't need browning first, so it can just be added straight to the pot, like the Scotch Broth (page 24), Braised Octopus with Herb Tabbouleh (page 56) or Irish Stew (page 99). Otherwise, if the meat needs to be browned, this can be done in another pan on the stove, and then, once the sauce is added, it can all be decanted into the slow cooker. The same goes for pressure cookers, which can be effective for dishes such as octopus or mutton, where plenty of moisture is vital to the finished dish. I'd choose a slow cooker over a pressure cooker, though, as they're more versatile. Although the flavour is never exactly the same as it is when you cook something slowly on the stove, since we're all short of time these days, what could be better than putting it all in the pot before you go to work and having a great meal ready on your return?

This book contains a large selection of recipes from all corners of the UK, which I hope will reignite some long-lost memories of your childhood. There are many international dishes here, too. As well as the very best comfort food, such as beef stew, the ultimate roast chicken and French onion soup, there are tips and surprises straight from some of the top chefs' kitchens. Cooking a fillet of beef at 80°C (175°F) in clingfilm is just one of these: it's completely foolproof and will wow your guests, and you'll never return to the old way of cooking beef again. Fish can benefit from the slow treatment, too, whether it's marinated, as in the treacle-cured salmon, or baked whole, as in the whole roast salmon with herbs. As a pastry chef for many years, it was a struggle for me to keep puddings and bakes out of a book on slow food! Meringues are always cooked slowly, and adding fresh strawberries to the mix makes all the difference. And it wouldn't be slow cooking without some proper puddings – there are plenty in here for you to enjoy, from classic custard tart to steamed ginger sponge.

Now you know what slow food is all about: proper honest grub that is as basic as cooking can get. I like to keep it simple, and this method of cooking gets rid of all the guesswork. It can be a great way to cook prime cuts of meat as well as the less well-known ones. I hope you enjoy it as much as I've enjoyed writing and cooking for it. Oh, and by the way: all the dishes were cooked and the photographs taken at my house, because I wanted to look forward to coming home as much as I used to when I was a kid. And I did!

Enjoy,

slow soups & broths

Whenever I go to Paris I make a beeline for a restaurant called Fouquet's on the Champs-Élysées. They serve the best French onion soup I've tasted. They add dry sherry, which makes all the difference, as does the amount of time you cook the onions before adding the stock. Simmering it slowly for at least an hour adds to the wonderful depth of flavour.

Serves 4

1.5kg white onions

4 fresh thyme sprigs

50g butter

4 tbsp olive oil

3 garlic cloves

75ml dry sherry

250ml white wine

3 tbsp plain flour

1.5 litres veal or beef stock

2 tsp soft brown sugar

4 thick slices white bread

250g Gruyère cheese, grated

sea salt and freshly ground
   black pepper

FRENCH ONION SOUP
WITH MELTED GRUYÈRE

Finely slice the onions and pick the leaves from the thyme sprigs. Heat a large sauté pan, add the butter, olive oil, onions and thyme and fry gently for 35–40 minutes over a medium-low heat, stirring occasionally, until softened and golden brown.

Finely chop the garlic cloves. When the onions are nearly cooked, add the garlic and cook for another couple of minutes. Add the sherry and white wine and simmer until they have reduced by half.

Add the flour, stirring constantly to get rid of any lumps, then cook for 1 minute. Add the stock and bring to a simmer, then cook gently for about 1 hour. Add the sugar and season with salt and pepper.

To make the croûtons, preheat the grill to high. Toast the bread in a toaster, then cut off the crusts. Cut the bread to fit the size of the flameproof bowls you plan to serve the soup in – it should be large enough to almost cover the soup with a small gap around the edge. Ladle the soup into the bowls, top with the toast and pile the cheese on top. Place under the grill until bubbling and golden brown. Serve immediately.

Tomato soup is one of the ultimate comfort foods, but roasting the tomatoes first give the dish a completely different taste, and by blending it with the skins you get a nice texture and flavour in the finished soup. Add a splash more double cream if it's a bit on the sharp side.

Serves 4

1.5kg ripe tomatoes

4 tbsp olive oil

1 large onion

2 garlic cloves

75g tomato purée

2 fresh thyme sprigs

50g caster sugar

1.5 litres vegetable stock

4 fresh coriander sprigs

100ml double cream (optional)

sea salt and freshly ground
  black pepper

ROASTED TOMATO SOUP

Preheat the oven to 180°C/350°F/Gas mark 4. Cut the tomatoes in half and place them in a large, deep roasting tray, then drizzle with the olive oil. Slice the onion, peel the garlic cloves and add to the tray. Spoon over the tomato purée, stir well to coat, then add the thyme and sugar. Roast in the oven for 1 hour.

When the tomatoes are cooked, put the vegetable stock in a large saucepan and bring to a simmer. Add the tomatoes and all the juices from the tray and stir to combine, then add the coriander. Ladle the tomatoes and liquid into a blender and purée in batches until smooth. Return to a large saucepan and return to a simmer. Season with salt and pepper and serve immediately, drizzling with double cream if you like.

It wasn't until I met the great American chef Thomas Keller that I got a masterclass in using maple syrup. Think of it like olive oil – you get what you pay for in terms of flavour, so it's worth shopping around. If you can find it, the syrup matured in bourbon barrels is the best I've ever tasted. Good-quality maple syrup is tapped directly from the tree by boring a hole in the trunk.

Serves 4

1kg parsnips

125g pecans

100ml maple syrup

2 litres vegetable or chicken stock

250ml milk

2 fresh tarragon sprigs

sea salt and freshly ground
  black pepper

PARSNIP, PECAN AND MAPLE SOUP

Cut the parsnips into into large, evenly sized chunks. Heat a large sauté pan or saucepan over a medium heat, add the pecans and toast for 1–1½ minutes, then tip out half of them and set aside.

Add the maple syrup to the remaining pecans and cook for another minute, stirring well, then add the parsnips and stir. Add the stock and milk, bring to a simmer and cook for 1 hour.

Remove from the heat, add the tarragon, then add to a blender in batches and process to a smooth purée. Return to the pan and heat gently to warm through, then season with salt and pepper. Roughly chop the reserved pecans. Ladle into bowls and serve with a few pecans scattered on top.

I love pumpkin. I often use it in desserts and even have pumpkin ice cream on the menu with a pineapple tarte tatin. But I use it in soup most of all, and roasting it first gives it an even better flavour. If you want a real winter warmer, add a dash of sherry or a few amaretti biscuits while it's in the blender.

Serves 4

1.5kg pumpkin or butternut squash

1 large onion

3 garlic cloves

4 tbsp olive oil

100g whole blanched almonds

1 litre vegetable or chicken stock

200ml double cream

3 tbsp spiced mixed nuts

2 tbsp extra-virgin olive oil

sea salt and freshly ground
   black pepper

ROAST PUMPKIN AND ALMOND SOUP

Preheat the oven to 180°C/350°F/Gas mark 4. Peel the pumpkin or squash and cut it into large chunks, and cut the onion into chunks. Place the pumpkin, onion and garlic on a large roasting tray, add the olive oil, season with salt and pepper and toss together well.

Roast in the oven for 50 minutes, then add the almonds and return to the oven for another 10 minutes. Place in batches into a blender, adding a little of the stock each time, and process to a purée. Pour into a saucepan over a medium heat. Add the cream, season with salt and pepper and bring to a simmer. Scatter with spiced nuts and a drizzle of extra-virgin olive oil, and serve hot or cold.

ds

ds

orns

3 garlic cloves

4 tbsp vegetable oil

4 tomatoes

1 fresh red chilli

1 tsp mustard seeds

6 curry leaves

4 tbsp fresh coriander leaves

4 tbsp Greek yoghurt

sea salt and freshly ground
black pepper

RED LENTIL SOUP

Place the lentils in a large saucepan with 2 litres water, the turmeric and salt. Heat a frying pan over a medium-high heat, break the dried chillies into pieces and add to the pan with the coriander, cumin and fenugreek seeds and black peppercorns. Toast for 20 seconds, stirring constantly. Remove and place in a pestle and mortar or spice grinder, then grind to a powder.

Finely chop the onion and garlic. Return the pan to the heat, then add 2 tablespoons of the vegetable oil, the onion and garlic, and cook gently for 10 minutes, until softened. Roughly chop the tomatoes. Add the spice mixture, onions and tomatoes to the lentils and bring to a simmer. Skim off and discard any scum, then cook for 1 hour over a very low heat, stirring from time to time.

Shortly before serving, slice the fresh chilli. Heat another frying pan until very hot and add the remaining vegetable oil. When the oil is smoking, add the mustard seeds, fresh chilli and curry leaves, then quickly remove from the heat. Finely chop the coriander. Remove any last residue of scum from the soup, then transfer it to a blender in batches and process until smooth. Return it to the pan to heat through and add the tempered spices and coriander. Season with salt and pepper. Ladle into serving bowls and finish with spoonfuls of yoghurt. Serve immediately.

This classic British soup from an old cookbook is thought to have been popular at Windsor Castle in the early twentieth century – and rightly so, because it's a fantastic winter warmer. Rice or bread were traditional thickeners for soups back then. You can use just beef or lamb, but I've used both here.

Serves 4

250g beef braising steak

250g lamb steak, trimmed of all fat

2 tbsp plain flour

25g butter

1 onion

1 carrot

1 parsnip

650ml fresh beef stock

1 fresh thyme sprig

1 bay leaf

1 small fresh rosemary sprig

200g cooked long-grain white rice

60ml Madeira

sea salt and freshly ground
  black pepper

BROWN WINDSOR SOUP

Cut the braising steak and lamb into 2.5cm dice. Place the diced meat in a mixing bowl, add the flour and toss together to thoroughly coat the meat. Place a heavy-based saucepan or casserole over a high heat and add the butter. When it starts to foam, add the meat and fry for 3–4 minutes, stirring occasionally, until dark golden brown.

Meanwhile, cut the onion, carrot and parsnip into dice. Add the vegetables to the pan and stir well, then add the stock, thyme, bay leaf and rosemary. Bring to the boil, cover and reduce the heat to a simmer. Cook gently for 1½ hours, until the meat is tender. To test this, cut into a piece of meat – if it flakes easily, it's ready.

Remove about 200ml of the cooked soup, including some of the meat and vegetables, and transfer to a blender. Process until smooth, then pour the purée back into the soup along with the cooked rice. Season with salt and pepper and serve with a splash of Madeira in each bowl.

Fennel is one of those vegetables that people either love or hate, and in the supermarket it seems to gather more dust than any other vegetable. But in Europe it's eaten a lot, often braised or thinly sliced in salads. I grow it in the garden and it's packed full of aniseed flavour. I especially love it in soups – the longer you cook it, the milder the flavour becomes.

Serves 4–6

2 shallots

2 garlic cloves

250g fennel

4 fresh thyme sprigs

3 tbsp olive oil

6 boneless and skinless
  chicken thighs

1.5 litres chicken stock

1 tsp fennel seeds

5 tomatoes

3 tbsp fresh flat-leaf parsley leaves

4 tbsp extra-virgin olive oil

sea salt and freshly ground
  black pepper

CHICKEN, FENNEL AND TOMATO SOUP

Roughly chop the shallots and garlic, and cut the fennel into 2cm dice. Pick the leaves from the thyme. Heat a large sauté pan until medium hot, add the olive oil, shallots, garlic, fennel and thyme and cook gently for 3 minutes, stirring occasionally, until softened but not coloured.

Meanwhile, cut the chicken into 2cm chunks. Increase the heat, add the chicken to the pan and fry until golden brown. Add the stock and bring to a gentle simmer. Cover with a lid and cook for 1 hour.

Meanwhile, heat a frying pan until hot, add the fennel seeds and toast for 30 seconds, then remove from the heat. Roughly chop the tomatoes and parsley. When the soup is cooked, add the fennel seeds and tomatoes and season with salt and pepper. Scatter with the parsley, drizzle with olive oil and serve.

As a northerner, I was brought up on this kind of food. My gran and auntie used to cook dishes like this, what I call fuel food. When we worked in the fields, coming back to a bowl of this gave us something to look forward to. It could be modernized, of course, but classic comfort food like this shouldn't be subjected to the sous-vide treatment, in my opinion. It's perfect for the slow cooker, though.

Serves 4–6

1kg lamb shoulder, on the bone

100g pearl barley

1 onion

2 carrots

1 swede

2 large potatoes

1 celery stick

½ Savoy cabbage

2 fresh thyme sprigs

1 litre chicken stock

1 fresh flat-leaf parsley sprig

sea salt and freshly ground
　black pepper

SCOTCH BROTH

Place the lamb in a large pan, cover with 2 litres water, then bring it to the boil over a medium heat. Reduce the heat to a gentle simmer and cook for 1½ hours, occasionally skimming off and discarding any foam on the liquid.

Put the pearl barley in a bowl, cover with cold water and set aside. Dice the onion, carrots, swede and potatoes into 1cm cubes. Cut the celery into 1cm lengths. Remove and discard the core from the cabbage, then thinly slice the leaves.

After 1½ hours, drain the pearl barley, discarding the water, and add it to the pan with the thyme and chicken stock, then simmer for a further 15 minutes. Next, add the onion, carrots, swede, celery and potatoes and continue to cook for 10 minutes. Add the cabbage and parsley and cook for a further 5 minutes.

Turn off the heat, carefully lift the lamb out from the liquid and place it on a chopping board. Using two forks, pull the meat from the bone and return it to the pan, discarding the bone. Stir well, season with salt and pepper, then serve.

When we think of lentils we usually think of India, but in fact nearly half the world's lentils are grown in Canada, including Puy lentils. Like all split pulses, they cook quickly and don't need soaking.

Serves 4–6

300g smoked streaky bacon

100g butter

1 onion

2 garlic cloves

3 fresh thyme sprigs

300g Puy lentils

150ml white wine

1 litre chicken stock

200g baby spinach leaves

4 thin pancetta slices

3 tbsp fresh flat-leaf parsley leaves

2 tbsp sherry vinegar

4 tbsp crème fraîche

sea salt and freshly ground
   black pepper

BACON AND PUY LENTIL SOUP

Roughly chop the bacon. Heat a large sauté pan or saucepan over a medium heat, add half the butter and the bacon and cook for 5–6 minutes, stirring occasionally, until golden brown. Meanwhile, roughly chop the onion and garlic and pick the leaves off the thyme. Add the onion, garlic and thyme to the pan and cook gently for another 15 minutes, until golden and soft.

Add the Puy lentils and white wine and simmer until reduced by half. Add the chicken stock and bring to a simmer. Cook for 1 hour over a gentle heat.

Meanwhile, heat a frying pan over a medium-high heat, add the remaining butter and the spinach and cook for 1–2 minutes, until wilted. Remove and place on kitchen paper to drain, then add the pancetta to the pan and fry on each side until golden and crisp. Place on kitchen paper to drain.

Roughly chop the parsley and add it to the soup along with the sherry vinegar. Season with salt and pepper. To serve, place some spinach in the centre of each soup plate. Ladle the soup around the spinach, then place a slice of pancetta on top of the spinach. Finish with a good dollop of crème fraîche.

Merguez sausages come from North Africa and the Middle East. They are made with lamb, beef or a mixture of the two, along with fennel seeds and garlic, but it's the chilli paste or harissa they contain that gives them the delicious kick and colour when they're cooked.

Serves 4

500g merguez sausages
2 shallots
2 garlic cloves
2 fresh red chillies
150ml white wine
400g cherry tomatoes

400g tinned haricot beans, drained
   and rinsed
1.5 litres chicken stock
6 tbsp fresh basil leaves
2 tbsp extra-virgin olive oil
sea salt and freshly ground
   black pepper

CHILLI, MERGUEZ SAUSAGE AND TOMATO SOUP

Cut the merguez sausages into 2cm chunks. Heat a large sauté pan or flameproof casserole dish over a medium-high heat, add the merguez sausages and fry for 3–4 minutes, stirring occasionally, until golden brown. Meanwhile, roughly chop the shallots and garlic and finely chop the chillies. Reduce the heat, then add the shallots, garlic and chillies and cook gently for 10 minutes, until softened but not coloured.

Add the white wine and simmer until reduced by half, then add the cherry tomatoes and cook for 3–4 minutes, squashing them down with the back of the spoon. Add the beans and stock and bring to a gentle simmer, then cover and cook for 1 hour. Once cooked, roughly chop the basil. Season the soup with salt and pepper. Scatter with the basil and drizzle with olive oil just before serving.

The first time I made consommé was at college, and I haven't seen it on many menus since. A lot of chefs are now turning to old recipe books to get ideas for new dishes, though. To go forwards sometimes you have to go back, and this is a classic. Full of flavour, it's a great dinner party dish – a little tricky to make, perhaps, but definitely worth it. You can now buy good fresh chicken stock at the supermarket, which is a lot easier to clarify.

Serves 4–6

2 roasted pheasant carcasses

3 carrots

2 leeks

1 fresh thyme sprig

3 egg whites

10g salt

3 litres chicken stock

1.5kg lean minced beef

10g truffles, or a drizzle of truffle oil

100g pheasant meat, minced

100ml double cream

2 tbsp fresh flat-leaf parsley leaves

150g cooked pearl barley

sea salt and freshly ground
   black pepper

GEORGE V CONSOMMÉ

Roughly chop the pheasant carcasses into 5cm pieces. Dice the carrots and leeks and remove the leaves from the thyme. Whisk the egg whites until lightly foamy. Place the salt, egg whites and stock into a bowl and whisk together well. Heat a large saucepan over a medium heat, then add the beef, pheasant carcasses, carrots, leeks and thyme and cook for about 5 minutes, until golden.

Add the stock and egg white mixture to the pan, stir well and bring to a gentle simmer, then cook for about 1½ hours, without stirring. The egg whites will form a crust on top of the broth that removes impurities and clarifies it. Pass the liquid through a sieve lined with a clean cloth or muslin into a clean saucepan, discarding the meat and vegetables.

Finely chop the truffles, if using. Put the pheasant meat in a bowl and slowly add the cream, stirring with a wooden spoon until it is all incorporated, then add the truffles and season with salt and pepper.

Return the clear broth to the heat and gently warm it through. Finely chop the parsley. Using a dessertspoon, shape the pheasant mixture into little balls or quenelles, then place them into the broth. Simmer for 2–3 minutes, then remove and place them in the serving bowls along with the pearl barley and parsley. Ladle the consommé over the top and serve immediately, drizzled with truffle oil, if using.

'Pepper water' is the original name for this Indian dish, which has been Anglicized over the years. It was traditionally thickened with rice, but I've used potatoes because I think the flavour is better. This is real comfort food, and the addition of rice makes it a meal in its own right.

Serves 4

½ onion

3 tbsp vegetable oil

2 garlic cloves

a 5cm piece of fresh ginger

200g potatoes

1 medium carrot

3 tomatoes

1 tsp ground cinnamon

2 tbsp Madras curry powder

1 litre chicken stock

200ml coconut milk

juice of 1 lime

100g cooked basmati rice

75g cooked mini poppadoms

4–6 tbsp mango chutney

sea salt and freshly ground
  black pepper

MULLIGATAWNY SOUP WITH CHUTNEY AND POPPADOMS

Finely dice the onion. Heat a large saucepan or sauté pan until hot, add the oil and onion and cook over a medium-low heat for 15 minutes, stirring, until very soft and lightly coloured. Meanwhile, crush the garlic and grate the ginger, then roughly chop the potatoes, carrot and tomatoes.

Add the garlic and ginger to the pan and cook for 2 minutes, then add the cinnamon and curry powder and cook for 1 minute. Add the potatoes, carrot and tomatoes and stir well. Add the chicken stock and bring to the boil, then reduce the heat to a very low simmer, cover and cook for 1 hour.

Using a blender, process the soup in batches until very smooth, then return to the pan. Add the coconut milk and lime juice and return to the heat. Taste and season with salt and pepper if necessary. Spoon the cooked rice into a soup plate, then pour the soup around it. Place the poppadoms and mango chutney on top of the rice.

slow vegetables

Like the Chicory and Ham Gratin on the next page, this is a French café dish that goes well with most meats and fish, or even with a fried egg. It can also be eaten cold. It comes from the Basque region of south-west France and is thought to resemble the Basque flag. It usually includes green peppers, but I think red have a nicer flavour and work better if you are going to use it as a garnish. It's great with the Treacle-glazed Ham Hocks (page 114) or the Sticky Chilli-braised Beef Ribs (page 145).

Serves 4

8 red peppers

2 garlic cloves

1 tsp tomato purée

1 tsp fennel seeds

50g caster sugar

3 tbsp red wine vinegar

400g tinned chopped tomatoes

6 large fresh basil leaves

3 tbsp olive oil

sea salt and freshly ground
   black pepper

OVEN-BAKED PIPERADE

Preheat the oven to 180°C/350°F/Gas mark 4. Cut the peppers into quarters, remove and discard the seeds, then cut each quarter in half lengthways. Lightly crush the garlic cloves.

Place the peppers, garlic, tomato purée, fennel seeds and sugar in a roasting tray and toss well to combine. Pour over the red wine vinegar and chopped tomatoes and stir again, then cover with foil and cook in the oven for 1 hour. Remove the foil and cook for a further 15 minutes.

When the peppers are soft, remove them from the oven. Finely shred the basil leaves and sprinkle over the top, then stir in the olive oil. Check the seasoning and serve hot or warm, or they can be cooled and stored in a sterilized preserving jar. Sealed, they'll keep for 2 months, and once opened they'll keep for 1–2 weeks in the fridge.

To sterilize jars, wash them with hot, soapy water, then place them in an oven preheated to 100°C/200°F/Gas mark ¼ for 30 minutes. Carefully remove with a clean cloth, being careful not to touch the insides, and allow to cool slightly before filling. Cover the contents with a circle of waxed paper, seal with the lid and store in a cool place.

I learnt this in a little French bistro in Paris, the kind of place with cheap, tasty food and lots of locals. I go there every time I'm in town and eat this dish with grilled chicken or beef – I love it! Following a quick tour around the kitchen and a masterclass from the French grandmother who cooks it, here it is.

Serves 4

75g butter

50g plain flour

500ml milk

1 tsp Dijon mustard

200g Gruyère or Emmental cheese, grated

4 large heads chicory

8 slices cooked ham

sea salt and freshly ground black pepper

CHICORY AND HAM GRATIN

Melt 50g of the butter in a heavy-based pan. Once it's bubbling slightly, add the flour and cook, stirring, for 2 minutes. Then, change the spoon for a whisk and add the milk a little at a time, whisking well to stop lumps forming, until you have a smooth sauce. Simmer the sauce gently for 4 minutes, then add the mustard and half the cheese, and season well with salt and pepper. Cover and set aside.

Preheat the oven to 170°C/325°F/Gas mark 3. Cut the chicory in half lengthways and season it with salt and pepper. Heat a frying pan until hot and add the remaining butter. When it bubbles, add the chicory cut-side down and fry for 1 minute, until just coloured. Remove from the pan and wrap each chicory half in a slice of ham, then place them in an ovenproof dish. Pour over the cheese sauce, cover with foil and bake for 40 minutes.

Remove the foil, sprinkle with the remaining grated cheese and return to the oven for 20 minutes, until golden brown. Serve hot and bubbling.

I always have marrows in the garden, mostly because I never seem to get through the amount of courgettes I plant each year. This fantastic recipe is how I use them all up. I've got so many I think I'm going to start looking like one, at this rate. Carrots for next season, I think.

Makes 500g

2kg marrow

1.5kg granulated sugar

50g fresh ginger

10 green cardamom pods

MARROW, GINGER AND CARDAMOM PRESERVE

Peel and deseed the marrow, then cut it into rough dice and place it on a tray. Sprinkle the sugar over the marrow, cover with clingfilm and place another tray on top, with a small tin on top of it to weight it down. Place in the fridge and leave overnight.

The next day, place the marrow, sugar and any juices into a large saucepan and bring to a gentle simmer over a medium heat. Cook until the marrow is translucent – about 1 hour.

Peel and grate the ginger, split the cardamom pods and scrape the seeds out. Add both to the saucepan and continue to cook for 5 minutes. Remove from the heat and allow to cool slightly. Pour into clean, sterilized preserving jars (see page 35). Seal and allow to cool completely before using. It will keep unopened for 2–3 months, and for 2 weeks in the fridge once opened.

This is a great way of using up wild mushrooms, and of preserving them when the season ends. It also works with chestnut or even small button mushrooms, and you can use white wine vinegar with a sprig of tarragon if you don't have tarragon vinegar. Serve warm with roast duck, chicken, venison or even chicken livers. They're also delicious cold with a pâté or terrine.

Makes 1 kg

200g oyster mushrooms

200g girolle mushrooms

200g pied bleu mushrooms

200g brown enoki mushrooms

200g chanterelle mushrooms

PICKLING SOLUTION:

250ml rice wine vinegar

2 tbsp tarragon vinegar

4 tsp demerara sugar

1 tsp flaky sea salt

2 star anise pods

1 cinnamon stick

PICKLED WILD MUSHROOMS

Keeping the mushrooms in separate piles, clean them by brushing them with a pastry brush around the gills to remove any excess dirt. Trim off the ends of the stalks.

For the pickling solution, place all the ingredients with 100ml water in a saucepan over a medium heat and cook until the sugar has dissolved. Remove from the heat, place the mushrooms into a sterilized preserving jar or large jam jar (see page 35) and pour the pickling solution over the top. Shake lightly to combine them well. Seal the jar and leave for about 1 week, turning the jars over every now and again. It will keep unopened for 2 months, and for 1–2 weeks in the fridge once opened.

This interpretation of a classic potato dauphinoise is a great dish for dinner parties. To make the presentation smarter, you can place a tray that just fits inside the dish on top of the dauphinoise when it comes out of the oven, weight it down with tins or bags of sugar and leave it to cool completely, then chill in the fridge. Cut it out into rounds with a cookie cutter, place on a baking tray and reheat in a hot oven.

Serves 6–8

1 garlic clove

50g butter

500g King Edward potatoes

500g white turnips

300ml double cream

300ml full-fat milk

pinch of freshly grated nutmeg

sea salt and freshly ground
  black pepper

POTATO AND TURNIP DAUPHINOISE

Preheat the oven to 170°C/325°F/Gas mark 3. Cut the garlic clove in half, then rub it around the inside of an ovenproof dish. Grease the dish with a little of the butter. Thinly slice the potatoes and turnips into a bowl. Season with salt and pepper and toss together well. Tip them into the prepared dish, pressing the slices down so that you end up with an even layer.

Pour the cream and milk into a large jug and whisk to combine. Season with salt, pepper and nutmeg and pour the cream and milk over the potatoes and turnips. Dot with the remaining butter, then cover tightly with foil. Cook in the oven for 1 hour, until the potatoes are tender.

After an hour, carefully remove the foil and return to the oven for a further 30 minutes, until golden brown on top.

2 cinnamon sticks

¼ tsp ground cloves

1 star anise pod

3 tbsp red wine vinegar

6 tbsp redcurrant jelly

sea salt and freshly ground
 black pepper

¡PICED RED CABBAGE
.LOTS

Peel the shallots and leave them whole. The best way to do this is to place them in a heatproof bowl, pour over a kettleful of boiling water, leave to stand for 5 minutes, then drain them. Once cooled, the skins will slip off more easily. Heat a large heavy-based pan over a medium-high heat, add a little of the butter and the shallots and cook for 3–4 minutes, until golden, then remove from the pan. Finely slice the red cabbage.

Add the remaining butter and the red cabbage and fry for 1–2 minutes, or until just softened. Add the red wine, bring to the boil, then lower the heat to a simmer and cook until reduced by half. Add the remaining ingredients (except the redcurrant jelly), and the browned shallots. Bring to a simmer, then cover and cook for 50 minutes, stirring occasionally, until tender.

Remove the lid, add the redcurrant jelly and cook for a further 5–8 minutes over a high heat, or until most of the liquid has evaporated and the cabbage is slightly sticky and glossy. Season with salt and pepper and serve.

My gran was the first person I remember baking whole onions, and it's good to see that they're now appearing on menus more often. Keeping the skins on during cooking helps the onions keep their shape. Vary the stuffing as much as you like, and you could use smaller onions for a fantastic accompaniment for roast chicken. It's a great dish for vegetarians, too, if you replace the bacon with chestnuts. The cooking time will be the same.

Serves 4

4 large white onions, skin on

4 rashers streaky bacon

3 tbsp fresh flat-leaf parsley leaves

80g fine dried breadcrumbs

2 fresh rosemary sprigs

50g butter, melted, plus extra
  for greasing

2 tsp sugar

sea salt and freshly ground
  black pepper

BAKED WHOLE ONIONS WITH BACON AND ROSEMARY

Preheat the oven to 170°C/325°F/Gas mark 3 and line a roasting tray with greaseproof paper. Grease a large sheet of foil. Cut the tops off the onions about a third of the way down, leaving the roots attached (trim the roots if necessary). Scoop out about a third of the centre of each onion with a spoon and discard it along with the tops, then place the onions in the roasting tray.

Cut the bacon into 5mm slices to make lardons. Roughly chop the parsley. Place the breadcrumbs, parsley and rosemary into a food processor and process for 30 seconds until combined. Remove from the machine and transfer to a mixing bowl, then add the bacon and melted butter and mix together. Season with salt and pepper.

Sprinkle each onion with a little of the sugar, then divide the breadcrumb mixture between the 4 onions, packing it on top of the onion to re-create its original shape. Pour 200ml water around the onions, then cover with the greased foil and bake for 1 hour. After 45 minutes, remove the foil and return to the oven to allow them to brown. Serve hot or at room temperature.

This is the kind of food chefs love to eat. I like using pancetta, but dry-cured bacon will work as well. Taleggio cheese has been made since the tenth century in the caves of Val Taleggio, northern Italy. Not only is this cows' milk cheese good grilled on toast or stirred into risotto, but it also goes well with polenta.

Serves 4

4 large baking potatoes

1 tbsp olive oil

1 tsp flaky sea salt

105g sliced pancetta

200g Taleggio cheese

small bunch fresh chives

sea salt and freshly ground
   black pepper

BAKED POTATOES WITH PANCETTA AND TALEGGIO

Preheat the oven to 180°C/350°F/Gas mark 4. Prick the potatoes all over with a fork, rub them with olive oil and sprinkle over the flaky sea salt.

Place the potatoes on the top shelf and bake for 1 hour, or until tender (allow longer for very large potatoes). Remove and allow to cool slightly before cutting in half lengthways. Scoop out the centres, transfer to a bowl and crush lightly with a fork.

Heat a frying pan over a medium-high heat, add the pancetta and cook for 1–2 minutes on each side, until crispy and golden brown. Remove and drain on kitchen paper. Slice the Taleggio into thick slices and roughly chop half of it. Roughly chop the pancetta and add it to the crushed potatoes, along with the chopped Taleggio. Mix well and season with salt and pepper, then scoop the mixture into the potato shells. Top with the remaining Taleggio slices and return to the oven for 10 minutes to heat through.

Finely chop the chives and sprinkle them over the potatoes. Serve immediately with a crisp green salad.

Sherry and parsnips make a great combination, and this is delicious with game and most roast birds, even chicken. Chestnuts are available all year round in vacuum-sealed packs, which means they keep for longer. If you have any leftovers they can be blended to make a tasty soup.

Serves 4

100g cooked peeled chestnuts

1kg medium-sized parsnips

350ml dry sherry, such as fino
 or manzanilla

100g soft brown sugar

100g butter

sea salt and freshly ground
 black pepper

SLOW-ROAST PARSNIPS WITH SHERRY AND CHESTNUTS

Preheat the oven to 170°C/325°F/Gas mark 3. Roughly chop the chestnuts. Place the whole, unpeeled parsnips, sherry, 200ml water, sugar and butter into an ovenproof dish or roasting tin, season with salt and pepper and stir well to combine, making sure the parsnips are well coated. Roast for 1 hour, until golden and tender.

Baking in a salt crust is an age-old technique. Tom Kerridge from the brilliant Hand & Flowers pub in Marlow, Buckinghamshire, cooks potatoes in a salt-water crust. It's the egg white that holds the salt together during cooking to form a crust, and in doing so traps in the flavours. Beetroot is great cooked this way, but you could try it with whole celeriac too, which would need to be cooked for longer. Only use rock salt, never fine table salt.

Serves 4

300g rock salt

3 fresh thyme sprigs

2 egg whites

6 large beetroot, skins on
 and washed

10 large fresh dill sprigs

3–4 tbsp extra-virgin olive oil

SALT-BAKED BEETROOT

Preheat the oven to 170°C/325°F/Gas mark 3. Place the salt and thyme in a food processor and process for 1 minute to form a powder, then add the egg whites and process again for 3 seconds.

Line a roasting tray with greaseproof paper and place the beetroot on it, then cover each one with the salt and egg mixture so that the beetroot is completely covered. Bake in the oven for 2 hours.

When the beetroot is cooked, remove it from the oven and allow to cool slightly before cracking off the salt crust. Finely chop the dill. Peel the skin off the beetroot, cut it into wedges and mix it with the olive oil and chopped dill. Serve with smoked salmon, or as a vegetable accompaniment – it's great with roast beef or chicken.

I've been cooking with salsify all my life, and these days it's becoming more widely available to buy. The flavour is similar to oysters, which is why it's sometimes called oyster plant. If you have lots to prepare, it's best to wear gloves, as it can stain your hands. It's great in soups or with fish dishes. This recipe is particularly good alongside the Whole Roast Salmon with Fennel and Herbs (page 67) or the Slow-Roast Pork Shoulder (page 109).

Serves 4–6

1 lemon

2kg salsify

500ml rapeseed oil

1 large fresh lemon thyme sprig

sea salt

OIL-BRAISED SALSIFY

Preheat the oven to 140°C/275°F/Gas mark 1. Squeeze the lemon into a large bowl, then add 200ml water. One at a time, peel the salsify and cut them into 5cm batons, then place them straight into the lemon water. This will prevent the salsify from oxidizing and turning brown.

Heat an ovenproof pan until medium hot. Add the oil and lemon thyme and heat until the oil is just trembling. Drain the salsify and pat dry, then place in the pan. Cover with a lid or foil, then cook in the oven for 1 hour.

Remove the pan from the oven and allow to cool completely before removing the foil or lid. Drain the salsify from the oil (the oil can be reserved and reused). Heat a non-stick frying pan over a medium heat, add the salsify and fry on each side until golden brown. Remove, season with salt and serve immediately.

slow
fish

Serves 4

1kg octopus, cleaned

3 garlic cloves

finely grated zest and juice
   of 1 unwaxed lemon

3 fresh thyme sprigs

4 tbsp olive oil

200g small round shallots

2 bay leaves

1 tbsp tomato purée

1 tbsp caster sugar

275ml red wine

400g tinned chopped tomatoes

TABBOULEH:

100g bulghur wheat, soaked in cold
   water overnight

1 red onion

1 bunch fresh flat-leaf parsley

1 bunch fresh mint

finely grated zest and juice
   of 1 unwaxed lemon

1 pomegranate

50g flaked almonds

4 tbsp extra-virgin olive oil

sea salt and freshly ground
   black pepper

I haven't always been a fan of octopus, but when I was working in Crete recently I had some as tapas and I loved it. It was char-grilled on an open fire and served with olive oil and lemon. It was great, mainly because of the way they prepared it beforehand: they hung it on a clothes line outside the restaurant and air-dried it for 24 hours before cooking, and we can achieve a similar result in the freezer. It also works well in a slow cooker or pressure cooker: try cooking it in a slow cooker for 2–3 hours on medium, or for 30 minutes in a pressure cooker.

BRAISED OCTOPUS WITH HERB TABBOULEH

Freeze the octopus for at least 48 hours, then defrost it in the fridge overnight – this helps tenderize it. Rinse it well, then pat dry before cutting it into 5cm pieces. Thickly slice the garlic and place it in a bowl with the octopus, lemon zest and juice and thyme. Stir well and put in the fridge to marinate for 1 hour.

Peel the shallots. Heat a large sauté pan until hot, add the olive oil and shallots and cook for 5 minutes, until softened. Add the marinated octopus and sauté for 2–3 minutes, then add the bay leaves, tomato purée, sugar and red wine. Bring to the boil and cook until the wine has reduced by half. Add the tomatoes and bring back to a simmer, then cook gently for 1–1½ hours, until the octopus is very tender.

Meanwhile, make the tabbouleh. Drain the bulghur wheat well and put it in a large bowl. Finely chop the red onion and roughly chop the parsley and mint. Cut the pomegranate in half and remove the seeds. To do this, cut it in half, then hit the outside with a wooden spoon while holding it over a bowl – the seeds will fall out into the bowl. Combine all the tabbouleh ingredients in a bowl and stir well. Season with salt and pepper and serve with the octopus.

I had this dish in one of the most amazing restaurants I've ever been to, on the Amalfi coast in Italy. When it's as fresh as that one was, a huge sea bass cooked in salt is one of the true culinary delights. It's also incredibly easy. You can do it with other fish, too, although you'd need to adjust the cooking time depending on the size.

Serves 4–6

1kg sea salt

3 egg whites

1 x 2kg whole sea bass, scaled, gutted
  and cleaned

SALT-BAKED SEA BASS

Preheat the oven to 150°C/300°F/Gas mark 2. Place the salt in a food processor and blitz, then add the egg whites and process until well combined. Remove and set aside.

Line a roasting tin big enough to hold the fish with greaseproof paper. Place the whole fish on its side in the tray.

Spread the salt over the top of the fish, making sure it is completely covered. Use the edge of a spoon to mark scales all over the fish. Cook in the oven for 1 hour, then turn the oven off and leave the door slightly ajar for a further 10 minutes before taking out the fish.

Carefully remove the salt crust and use a pastry brush to sweep away any excess salt, taking care not to break the skin of the fish. Transfer to a serving dish and serve with lemon halves and a rocket and Parmesan salad.

Spain has some of the best ingredients in the world. Of all the amazing produce you can find in the markets there, the pork products have to be the best of the bunch. Chorizo sausage is made from pork, salt and pimentón peppers, which give it a fantastic smoky flavour and rich colour. Look out for the 'picante' (spicy) version, and try to buy soft cooking chorizo, rather than the dry-cured version, which is better for slicing.

Serves 4

250g cooking chorizo

2 banana shallots

2 garlic cloves

6 tomatoes

2 fresh thyme sprigs

400g tinned chickpeas, drained
  and rinsed

200ml white wine

500ml chicken stock

4 x 200g thick fillets halibut
  on the bone

2 tbsp fresh flat-leaf parsley leaves

sea salt and freshly ground
  black pepper

BRAISED HALIBUT WITH CHICKPEAS AND CHORIZO

Preheat the oven to 170°C/325°F/Gas mark 3. Slice the chorizo, thinly slice the shallots and crush the garlic cloves. Heat a flameproof casserole dish until medium hot, then add the chorizo and fry for 4–5 minutes, stirring occasionally, until the oil is released. Meanwhile, roughly chop the tomatoes. Add the shallots, garlic, thyme and tomatoes and cook for a further 3–4 minutes.

Add the chickpeas and stir well, then add the white wine and chicken stock and bring to the boil. Cover with the lid and bake in the oven for 1 hour, then remove and place the halibut on top of the chickpeas. Cover again and return to the oven for a further 15 minutes. Remove from the oven and allow to rest for 5 minutes before removing the lid. Roughly chop the parsley.

Carefully lift out the fish using a fish slice and place on a serving dish. Stir the parsley into the chickpeas, season with salt and pepper, and serve them alongside the fish.

Miso is one of those things people tend to walk past in the shop because they don't know what to do with it, but it's definitely worth a try. It's a Japanese flavouring paste made with fermented rice, barley or soya beans, which comes in brown or white varieties (either will do for this dish). The basting may seem like a bore but it does help give a rich, deep colour and flavour.

Serves 4

4 x 450g monkfish tails, trimmed

75ml sake

75ml mirin

200g miso paste

100g granulated sugar

MISO-MARINATED MONKFISH

Trim the monkfish tails so that the bone sticks out at least 3cm from the flesh, then wrap the bone in foil (you can use any trimmings in a fish pie). Put the sake and mirin in a saucepan and bring to the boil. Boil for 20–30 seconds to burn off the alcohol, then reduce the heat, add the miso paste and stir to dissolve. Increase the heat and add the sugar, stirring well until it dissolves. Remove from the heat and pour into a roasting tin big enough to hold the monkfish tails.

Allow to cool completely, then add the monkfish tails and toss to coat thoroughly in the miso mixture. Cover and place in the fridge for at least 24 hours, preferably 48, turning occasionally.

Preheat the oven to 150°C/300°F/Gas mark 2. Turn the monkfish to make sure it's completely covered in the miso, reserving any excess marinade. Roast in the oven for 1 hour, turning and basting every 20 minutes or so with the reserved miso marinade. Remove and allow to rest for 10 minutes before serving.

2 whole mackerel, filleted, skinned and pin bones removed

2 shallots

1 red chilli

2 garlic cloves

250ml malt vinegar

1 bay leaf

½ tsp fennel seeds

½ tsp cumin seeds

½ tsp black peppercorns

finely grated zest and juice of 1 unwaxed lemon

POTATOES AND WATERCRESS:

300g cooked new potatoes

2–3 tbsp olive oil

2 bunches watercress

1 tbsp sultanas

sea salt and freshly ground black pepper

I love pickled fish: prepared nicely, it's one of the best ways of showing off the flavour. Mackerel is a great fish and we should all eat more of it, instead of relying on the usual cod and haddock. It's best eaten fresh, and pickling it means you can preserve all that delicious flavour in the fish.

PICKLED MACKEREL WITH POTATOES AND WATERCRESS

Place the mackerel fillets in a shallow ovenproof dish, flesh-side down. Set aside. Thinly slice the shallots, deseed and finely dice the chilli and crush the garlic cloves. Place them in a saucepan along with the vinegar, bay leaf, spices, lemon zest and juice, and 125ml water. Heat gently to warm through, then pour the liquid over the mackerel. Cover with foil and leave to marinate for 1 hour in the fridge.

Meanwhile, cut the potatoes in half and place them in a mixing bowl. Season with salt and pepper and drizzle with a little of the oil, stir together lightly and set aside. Pick the leaves from 1 bunch of watercress (reserving the stalks) and set aside.

Prepare a bowl of cold water with ice. Bring a pan of water to the boil, add a pinch of salt, then add the second bunch of watercress and the stalks from the first bunch, and cook for 20 seconds. Remove and plunge into the ice-cold water. Using your hands, squeeze most of the water out of the watercress and place it in a blender. Process to a fine purée, adding a little of the cooking water if necessary, and set aside.

To serve, spoon a little of the watercress purée into the centre of the plate and spread it out to form a circle using the back of the spoon. Scatter the potatoes on top, along with the watercress leaves. Lift the mackerel fillets out of the marinade and place on top of the salad. Sprinkle with the sultanas and spoon a little of the mackerel pickling liquor over the top. Finish with a drizzle of oil.

The word gravadlax (or gravlax) is thought to come from the Swedish word 'grav', meaning grave. 'Lax' means salmon, so all together it means buried salmon. It was a method of preservation that fishermen used to do by salting the salmon and burying it under the sand. Times have moved on, so there's no need to get out your bucket and spade – you just need time to let the sugar and salt do their work. Once you've made it the first time you'll soon realize how easy it is to prepare.

Serves 8–10

2 vanilla pods

250g flaky sea salt

150g caster sugar

2 x 900g thick salmon fillets, skin on, scaled and pin bones removed

2 large bunches fresh dill

2 tbsp Dijon mustard

2 handfuls watercress leaves

3 tbsp olive oil

SALMON GRAVADLAX

Slit the vanilla pods in half lengthways, scrape out the seeds and cut the pods into pieces. Put the salt, sugar, vanilla seeds and pods in a food processor and blitz for 30 seconds. Find a large, shallow, rectangular dish or roasting tin big enough for the salmon to lie flat and line it with clingfilm, leaving plenty hanging over the sides.

Sprinkle a third of the curing mixture over the bottom of the dish and spread it over the base. Put one of the salmon fillets on top, skin-side down. Sprinkle another third of the curing mixture and place the other fillet on top, skin-side up, on top. Sprinkle the remaining curing mixture on top and fold the clingfilm over them. Place in the fridge for 6 hours.

Finely chop the dill. Rinse the curing mixture off the salmon with cold water and pat it dry with kitchen paper. Spread the mustard over the flesh side of the salmon, then sprinkle it with dill. Cover it very tightly with clingfilm and place in the fridge for 2 hours.

Remove the gravadlax from the clingfilm and slice into thin slices. Drizzle the watercress leaves with the oil and serve alongside the gravadlax.

Roasting on the bone is a great way to cook fish, as it keeps it nice and moist. Cooking it whole also helps hold it together if you do overcook it slightly. You can vary the flavours you put inside the fish, but keeping it simple works best.

Serves 8–10

1 bulb fennel

25g fresh dill

25g fresh flat-leaf parsley

2 garlic cloves

1 tsp fennel seeds

1 lemon

3–3.5kg whole salmon, gutted,
  cleaned and scaled

200ml white wine

sea salt and freshly ground
  black pepper

WHOLE ROAST SALMON WITH FENNEL AND HERBS

Preheat the oven to 170°C/325°F/Gas mark 3. Line a roasting tin big enough to hold the salmon with greaseproof paper. Thinly slice the fennel, chop the dill and parsley and crush the garlic. Mix them all together in a bowl with the fennel seeds. Thinly slice the lemon.

Season the salmon well with salt and pepper, then place it on its side, open the cavity and spread out the fennel mixture inside the fish, followed by the sliced lemon. Place the salmon in the tin with the stuffed cavity facing down. Pour over the wine, then cover with greased foil and cook in the oven for 1 hour.

Remove the foil and baste the salmon with the cooking liquid, then return to the oven for a further 15 minutes. Remove and allow to stand for 3–4 minutes before serving. It can be served hot or cold.

Black treacle isn't used much in cooking because of its strong flavour – in fact, the only other time I use it is in sticky toffee pudding. But here it produces a wonderful cured salmon, the treacle adding both colour and flavour.

Serves 6

800g salmon fillet, skin on, pin bones
    removed, washed and patted dry
150g sea salt

100g caster sugar
200ml whisky
100g black treacle

TREACLE-MARINATED SALMON

Place 4 pieces of clingfilm, slightly overlapping, on a clean work surface, then place the salmon fillet on top, skin-side down. Mix the salt and sugar together in a bowl, then cover the salmon with it, packing it down firmly. Wrap the salmon up tightly with the clingfilm, then place it on a tray. Place a couple of packs of butter or another light weight on top to gently press down on the salmon, then put it in the fridge and leave for about 8 hours.

Remove the salmon from the clingfilm, brush off the salt mixture and rinse it thoroughly under cold water, then pat dry. Line the same tray with more clingfilm and place the salmon in the centre.

Pour over the whisky and wrap in clingfilm again, then return to the fridge for a further 3 hours. After this time, unwrap the clingfilm, lift the salmon out of the whisky and place it on a board. Warm the black treacle in a small pan until just runny, then brush it over the top of the fillet to cover it evenly. Wrap it one last time in clingfilm and return to the fridge for 1 hour. Carve into thin slices to serve. It's good with a salad of Little Gem leaves and some brown bread.

One of the things I love about Asian cooking is the combination of flavours, and the simplicity of them when brought together in a dish. Rice wine vinegar is best for this, and the dressing can be used on salads too. We often make this dish for large parties, as it's so simple to serve and tastes great. We sometimes cube it, but slices are fine too, as the pickling liquid cures the fish in one piece.

Serves 8–10

1 x 1kg salmon fillet, skinned and pin
   bones removed

500ml rice wine vinegar

50g caster sugar

50g sea salt

2 garlic cloves

25g fresh ginger

1 unwaxed lemon

3 limes

1 cucumber

4 fresh mint sprigs

4 fresh dill sprigs

1 punnet salad or coriander cress
   (optional)

150ml rapeseed oil

PICKLED SALMON WITH CUCUMBER AND MINT

Trim any brown meat off the salmon. Rinse it and pat dry with kitchen paper, then place it in a dish large enough to hold it flat, and set aside. Put the vinegar in a saucepan, add the sugar and salt and gently heat until dissolved. Do not allow it to boil. Remove from the heat and grate in the garlic and ginger, then allow to cool. Zest 1 of the lemons and 1 of the limes and set the zest aside, then juice all the lemons and limes.

When the vinegar solution has cooled completely, add the lemon and lime juice and stir well to combine. Remove 75ml of the liquid and set aside, then pour the rest over the salmon and cover the tray with clingfilm. Leave to marinate in the fridge for at least 48 hours. After 48 hours, remove from the fridge, take the salmon out of the liquid, and discard the liquid. Pat the fish dry with kitchen paper and slice it as thinly as possible, or cut it into small cubes. Place it on a serving plate.

Using a small melon baller or Parisienne scoop, cut little balls out of the cucumber and scatter them over the salmon (you can cut it into cubes if you don't have a melon baller). Finely shred the mint and dill, then scatter them over the top with the reserved lemon and lime zest, and the salad or coriander cress, if using. Put the reserved vinegar solution in a small blender and process it slowly, adding the rapeseed oil gradually until it emulsifies to make a dressing. Drizzle it over the salmon and serve.

This dish is really clever, and I've got my team to thank for it. They were on a roll, and I had to stop them stuffing eight fish inside each other! The idea comes from a traditional dish in which game birds are boned and stuffed inside one another. It looks tricky, but it's really quite simple, and fish is far easier to work with than game. You could use greaseproof paper in place of the banana leaf. For a more economical version, try adapting the recipe with salmon, red mullet or sea bass, and mackerel. Ask your fishmonger to butterfly the fish for you.

Serves 8–10

3 x 60cm sheets banana leaf

90g butter

1 x 2.5kg salmon, cleaned, gutted and pin bones removed

6 tbsp fresh chervil sprigs

1 x 1.5–1.7kg sea bass, head removed and butterflied

4 tbsp fresh flat-leaf parsley leaves

3 x 600g cooked lobsters, shelled

sea salt and freshly ground black pepper

A FISH INSIDE A FISH

Preheat the oven to 170°C/325°F/Gas mark 3. Place the banana leaves on a large baking tray, overlapping slightly. Thickly slice the butter.

Place the salmon lengthways on the banana leaves and season with salt and pepper. Place half the butter slices over the flesh, then scatter the chervil sprigs in the cavity.

Place the sea bass skin-side down inside the salmon cavity on top of the chervil, then season with salt and pepper. Add the remaining butter and scatter over the parsley leaves. Place the lobster meat in a line down the centre of the sea bass. Fold the salmon over the sea bass so that it looks like a whole fish again.

Lifting it off the banana leaves slightly, tie the salmon at 10cm intervals with kitchen string to hold its shape. Fold the banana leaves over the salmon, then roll up into a cylinder and tie both ends with string to secure it. Place on a baking tray and roast in the oven for 1 hour.

Remove and allow to rest for 10 minutes before serving. It's great with a simple, crisp green salad, some crème fraîche flavoured with lemon juice, and crusty bread.

slow
one-pots

This classic dish from the Rhône-Alpes region of France, near the border with Italy, is a meal in itself. As well as being known for this dish, the Rhône-Alpes was also where the first Winter Olympics was held. Skiing isn't my idea of fun, but this is certainly a very good dish!

Serves 4

1.5kg medium-sized all-purpose potatoes, such as Desiree

1 large onion

4 thick dry-cured smoked streaky bacon rashers

50g butter

1 garlic clove

1 x 250g petit Reblochon cheese

sea salt and freshly ground black pepper

TARTIFLETTE

Preheat the oven to 180°C/350°F/Gas mark 4. Put the potatoes, unpeeled, in a large pan, cover with water, bring to the boil and cook for 15 minutes. Meanwhile, finely dice the onion and bacon. Melt the butter in a heavy-based pan over a low heat, add the onion and bacon and cook gently for 10 minutes, stirring occasionally, until softened but not coloured.

Drain the potatoes and let them cool a little. As soon as you can, peel them and cut into slices about 5mm thick. Cut the garlic clove in half and rub the inside of an ovenproof dish or baking tin with it. Place some of the potato slices over the base of the dish, season with salt and pepper and sprinkle with some of the bacon and onion. Keep layering the potatoes, bacon and onion and continue until all the potatoes have been used up, seasoning between each layer.

Trim the sides of the petit Reblochon all the way around, removing about 5mm of the skin. Place the cheese on the top of the potatoes and cover tightly with foil. Bake in the oven for 1 hour, until the potatoes are crisp around the edges and the cheese is well melted. Remove the foil and cook for a further 15 minutes, or until it is just crispy around the edges. Serve on its own or with a dressed green salad.

Squid is one of those types of seafood which, like octopus, either needs very quick cooking or long, slow cooking. Most of the squid you find in the shops tends to be large, and that's why it's suited to this kind of recipe. I count myself among the many people who don't cook squid at home as much as they should, but it's very popular in restaurants so I've come up with a recipe that's not at all fussy to make at home. This is tasty hot or cold.

Serves 4

1kg medium-sized squid

2 onions

3 garlic cloves

2 red peppers

75ml olive oil

1 tbsp tomato purée

150ml red wine

400g tinned chopped tomatoes

150g pitted black olives, drained

1 tbsp red wine vinegar

juice of 1 lemon

2 handfuls fresh basil leaves

sea salt and freshly ground
   black pepper

BRAISED SQUID WITH TOMATOES AND OLIVES

Preheat the oven to 140°C/275°F/Gas mark 1. Clean the squid by pulling off the tentacles and discarding any innards. Pull off and discard the outer membrane and the fins. Rinse well under cold water if necessary, pat dry with kitchen paper and cut into large triangles.

Cut the onions and garlic into thick slices. Deseed and slice the peppers. Heat a large frying pan until medium hot, add the olive oil, onions, garlic and peppers and sweat for a few minutes until softened, then add the squid and stir well. Add the tomato purée and red wine, bring to the boil and simmer until reduced by half, then add the tinned tomatoes and olives and stir well.

Cover with a lid or foil, then cook in the oven for 1 hour. Remove from the oven and take off the lid. Stir in the red wine vinegar, lemon juice and basil leaves, season with salt and pepper and serve with crusty bread.

This is one of my favourite recipes in the whole book – I just love the flavours in it. Cooking the chicken whole makes it even more succulent, but you can also do it with chicken pieces. Pheasant and partridge are great cooked this way too, but will only need 30–45 minutes.

Serves 4–6

1 onion

2 garlic cloves

6 smoked streaky bacon rashers

rapeseed oil, for frying

100g button mushrooms

125ml white wine

2 x 400g tins chopped tomatoes

1 litre brown chicken stock

2 tsp sugar

2 tbsp fresh tarragon leaves

400g new potatoes

1 x 2kg chicken, giblets removed

sea salt and freshly ground
  black pepper

POT-ROAST CHICKEN WITH HUNTERS' SAUCE

Preheat the oven to 170°C/325°F/Gas mark 3. Cut the onion, garlic and bacon into large dice. Place a 3-litre flameproof casserole dish over a medium heat. Add a little oil, then the bacon and fry until golden brown. Add the onion and garlic and cook for 2 minutes, until softened.

Slice the mushrooms thickly, add to the pan and fry for a further minute. Add the wine and tomatoes, bring to the boil and simmer for 3 minutes, then add the stock. Bring back to the boil and season with salt, pepper and sugar. Chop the tarragon and add half of it to the pan, reserving the rest.

Cut the potatoes into 1cm slices and add them to the pan. Place the chicken on top, pressing it down lightly to immerse it in the stock, then cover with a lid and cook in the oven for 1½ hours. After 1 hour, remove the lid and baste the chicken with the sauce. Return to the oven, uncovered, to allow the chicken to brown.

When the chicken is cooked, remove it and place on a chopping board. Leave to rest for 5 minutes. Add the remaining tarragon to the sauce, stir well and taste to check the seasoning. Carve the chicken into portions: cut the legs off, cut through the joint to separate the drumsticks from the thighs, and carve the breasts off the carcass. Place on a serving dish, then spoon the sauce and potatoes over the chicken.

This dish uses the fantastic produce I found in one of the many brilliant markets around Spain, and I ate it a lot while I was out there recently. 'Picante' cooking chorizo is the type to look for, as it's full of flavour and spice. The Spanish wood-roasted red piquillo peppers you can buy in jars can be added too. Adding some new potatoes to the pot makes it a perfect one-pot meal, or eat it with crusty bread and a green salad.

Serves 4

4 red peppers

350g cooking chorizo

1 x 1.5kg chicken, giblets removed

400ml white wine

40ml olive oil

SAUCE:

2 large or 3 small shallots

6 tbsp fresh flat-leaf parsley leaves

1 red chilli

1 green chilli

2 tbsp fresh oregano leaves

½ bunch fresh chives

2 tbsp sherry vinegar

2 tbsp olive oil

juice of 1 lemon

sea salt and freshly ground
  black pepper

CHICKEN WITH RED PEPPERS, CHORIZO AND CHILLI

Preheat the oven to 180°C/350°F/Gas mark 4. Deseed the peppers and cut them lengthways into 8 strips. Cut the chorizo into 1cm slices. Place the peppers and chorizo in a large casserole dish or roasting tin, then put the chicken on top. Pour the wine over, then drizzle with the olive oil and season with salt and pepper. Cover with a lid or foil and cook for 1 hour. Remove the foil or lid and cook for a further 30 minutes.

While the chicken is cooking, finely chop the shallots, parsley, red and green chillies, oregano and chives. Place all the sauce ingredients in a bowl, mix well, then season with salt and pepper. Pour the sauce ingredients over the chicken while it's in the pot, and take it to the table to serve.

Serves 8–10

HOT-WATER PASTRY:

100g butter, plus extra for greasing

100g lard

350g plain flour, plus extra
   for dusting

a pinch of sea salt

FILLING:

4 boneless, skinless duck breasts

2 banana shallots

2 garlic cloves

2 fresh thyme sprigs

a drizzle of rapeseed oil

3 boneless, skinless chicken breasts

2 egg whites

200ml double cream

100g hazelnuts, skinned

25g fresh flat-leaf parsley

sea salt and freshly ground
   black pepper

SOUSED CHERRIES:

300g cherries

75ml mirin

75ml rice vinegar

50g caster sugar

There aren't many things I find more enjoyable to cook than a simple pie, and I love hot-water crust pies most of all. Once you know how to make the pastry you can experiment with the fillings. The cherries work well, and figs would also be good.

DUCK AND CHICKEN PIE WITH SOUSED CHERRIES

Grease a 30 x 11cm springform or loose-bottomed loaf tin with butter, dust with flour and line the base with baking parchment. Place 2 long strips of folded-over foil in the tin lengthways, hanging over the edges, to help lift out the pie later. Now make the pastry. Cut the butter and lard into cubes. Bring the butter, lard, 75ml water and salt to the boil, then stir in the flour all at once to form a dough. Set aside to cool in the fridge for 30 minutes. Lightly flour a work surface and roll out the dough until it is 5mm thick. Cut into four 50 x 12cm rectangles. Place 3 pieces in the tin and gently push down into the corners, making sure it hangs over the edge. Put in the fridge to rest with the remaining pastry.

Cut the duck breasts lengthways into 3 strips and season with salt and pepper. Heat a non-stick frying pan until very hot and fry until golden brown, turning halfway. Remove and set aside. Dice the shallots and garlic. Heat the same frying pan, add a splash of oil and the shallot, garlic and thyme, and cook gently until softened. Remove from the heat and let cool.

Dice the chicken breast and place in a food processor with the egg whites, season with salt and pepper and process for about 1 minute. Add the cooked shallots and process again, then slowly add the cream. When it is well incorporated, transfer to a mixing bowl. Heat a frying pan until hot, add the hazelnuts and toast them lightly, then remove and roughly chop. Roughly chop the parsley, then add both to the chicken mixture.

Preheat the oven to 170°C/325°F/Gas mark 3. Spread out 1cm of the chicken mixture in the bottom of the tin, then place a duck breast piece on top. Repeat to make layers, pushing down gently to remove any air pockets, until the tin is filled. Place the last pastry piece on top and press the edges lightly to seal. Trim off any excess and crimp the edges. Bake in the oven for 1¼ hours. Check occasionally to ensure that the pastry is not browning too quickly – if it is, cover it with foil. To make the soused cherries, halve the cherries, put in a pan with the mirin, rice vinegar and sugar and bring to the boil. Cook until reduced by half, then set aside to cool. Let the pie cool for 15 minutes before lifting it out. Serve warm or cold, with the cherries.

I see all kinds of new ingredients on my television show, Saturday Kitchen, and Japanese umeboshi (pickled plum-like fruits) were a great discovery. They are available from large supermarkets or Asian food shops, and along with mirin (a sweetened rice wine), they taste great with duck and poultry. You can also buy banana leaves in Asian shops, and they freeze well too.

Serves 4

1 x 1kg guinea fowl, giblets removed

2 pieces stem ginger, plus a little of the syrup

150ml mirin

300g umeboshi

1 tsp salt

1 bunch spring onions

12 whole shiitake mushrooms

3 banana leaves

GUINEA FOWL WITH UMEBOSHI IN BANANA LEAF

Boil a kettle and pour the hot water over the guinea fowl (this tightens the skin and allows it to crisp). Allow to drain and set aside.

Place the stem ginger, ginger syrup, mirin, half the umeboshi and salt in a blender and process to form a paste. Remove and spread over the guinea fowl, then leave to marinate for 1 hour in the fridge.

Preheat the oven to 170°C/325°F/Gas mark 3. Trim the ends off the spring onions. Place 3 sheets of foil on a clean work surface, slightly overlapping, and place the banana leaves on top. Place the mushrooms in the centre of the banana leaf along with the remaining umeboshi, then place the spring onions on top of them.

Remove the guinea fowl from the fridge and place on top of the mushrooms, umeboshi and spring onions, then pour over any excess marinade. Carefully wrap the bird in the banana leaves, using the foil to seal it and form a parcel. Place in a roasting tin and cook in the oven for 1 hour. Remove from the oven and allow to stand for 10 minutes before opening the leaves at the table. Carve it as you would a chicken: cut the legs off, cut through the joint to separate the drumsticks from the thighs, and carve the breasts off the carcass.

Serves 4

500g stewing beef

50g plain flour

4 tbsp beef dripping or oil

100g celery

100g carrot

1 large leek

3 garlic cloves

150g whole baby onions

150ml red wine

500ml beef stock

3 tbsp fresh flat-leaf parsley leaves

sea salt and freshly ground
   black pepper

DUMPLINGS:

200g plain flour, plus extra
   for dusting

1½ tsp baking powder

a good pinch of salt

75g shredded suet

Browning the meat well is very important when making stews like this, so brown it in batches in a hot pan to make sure it doesn't braise. The meat should also be cut into decent-sized pieces, otherwise they'll cook too quickly. The larger the dice, the less fat you tend to find on it. Use beef dripping if you can – there's no olive oil or fancy stuff in this dish, which was my gran's favourite.

BEEF STEW WITH DUMPLINGS

Preheat the oven to 150°C/300°F/Gas mark 2. Toss the beef and flour together in a bowl with salt and pepper. Heat a large flameproof casserole dish until hot, add a little dripping or oil and enough of the beef to just cover the bottom of the casserole. Fry until browned on each side, then remove and set aside. Repeat with more dripping and beef in batches.

Meanwhile, cut the celery, carrot and leek into 2.5cm pieces and roughly chop the garlic. Add the last of the dripping and the onions, garlic, celery, carrot and leek, then cook gently for 5–10 minutes, until softened and lightly coloured. Return the beef to the casserole and add the red wine. Simmer until reduced by half, then add the beef stock and bring back to a simmer. Cover with a lid and place in the oven for 2 hours.

To make the dumplings, mix the flour, baking powder, salt and suet in a bowl and gradually add 3–5 tablespoons water, just enough to form a slightly sticky dough. Dust your hands with a little flour and roll the dough into small balls about the size of a ping-pong ball, then set aside.

After 2 hours, remove the stew from the oven and carefully place the dumplings on top. Return to the oven for 20 minutes, uncovered, until the dumplings have cooked through and turned light golden brown. Roughly chop the parsley and sprinkle over the stew to serve.

PASTRY:

60g cold lard or butter, plus extra
for greasing

225g self-raising flour, plus extra
for dusting

1 tsp salt

90g shredded beef suet

1 egg

FILLING:

1 onion

2 carrots

2 garlic cloves

rapeseed oil, for frying

750g boneless rabbit, diced

2 tbsp plain flour

125ml red wine

1 litre beef stock

1 fresh thyme sprig

100g hazelnuts, toasted

sea salt and freshly ground
black pepper

I first had this dish at a shoot lunch, and after a day in a cold field with the gun dogs it was just what I needed. If you're not fond of rabbit, other types of game, or beef, will work well too. The idea is that it's a self-contained meal, complete with proper gravy.

RABBIT, ALE AND HAZELNUT SUET PIE

To make the pastry, grate the lard or butter, then place it in a bowl with the flour, salt and suet and mix to combine. Add 150–175ml water to form a smooth dough, then knead it for a minute. Wrap it in clingfilm and put it in the fridge to rest for about 20 minutes.

Grease a 1-litre pudding basin with butter and dust it with flour. Roll out two-thirds of the pastry on a lightly floured work surface to about 2cm thick, allowing about 2cm extra all the way round the basin. Place the pastry into the basin and push it into the corners, making sure that there is an overhang around the edges. Roll out the rest of the pastry to make the lid for the pie and place it on a tray in the fridge to rest.

Dice the onion and carrots and crush the garlic. Heat a large saucepan over a medium heat, add a little oil and the onion and cook for 2 minutes without colouring, then add the garlic and cook for 1 more minute. Add the carrots and cook for 2–3 minutes, then drain into a colander.

Toss the rabbit with the flour so that it is well coated, season with salt and pepper, then return the pan to the heat and drizzle in a little more oil. Add the rabbit and fry on each side until golden brown. Add the red wine and simmer until reduced by half, then add the stock and thyme, bring to the boil, then reduce the heat to a simmer. Cook for 50 minutes.

Roughly chop the hazelnuts and add them to the cooked vegetables in the colander. After 35 minutes, add the vegetables to the pan with the rabbit and continue to cook for another 15 minutes. Remove from the heat and check the seasoning.

Preheat the oven to 170°C/325°F/Gas mark 3. Lightly beat the egg. Remove the pastry-lined pudding basin from the fridge and pour the rabbit filling into it. Brush the edges of the pastry with a little beaten egg and place the pastry lid on top, pressing together gently to seal it. Brush the top of the pie with the egg. Place on a cloth in a deep-sided roasting tin, then half-fill with water and cook in the oven for 1 hour. Remove and allow to stand for 10 minutes before serving.

This dish is a must for me, as my family were pig farmers, and it's from them that I got a real taste for pork. It's just so simple, and uses all the best parts of the pig. The recipe comes from a château kitchen in the south of France, where I was inspired by its pure, simple flavours. There's no need to be put off by making a terrine – it's very simple, and it's actually the dish it is cooked in (the terrine) that makes it easy for us. Serve it with pickles, chutney or gherkins and some crusty bread and butter.

Serves 10–12

300g pork liver

900g pork mince

120ml good white wine

6 tbsp Armagnac

16 thin back bacon rashers

2 eggs

100ml double cream

1 tsp sea salt

1 tsp freshly ground black pepper

a good pinch of ground nutmeg

3 fresh thyme sprigs

PORK AND ARMAGNAC TERRINE

First, the meat needs to marinate for 24 hours before cooking. Cut the pork liver into dice, place in a food processor and process to a purée. Combine with the pork mince in a large bowl, pour over the wine and Armagnac, mix well, cover with clingfilm and place in the fridge overnight.

The next day, preheat the oven to 140°C/275°F/Gas Mark 1. Line the sides and the base of a 30 x 11cm terrine with the bacon, allowing it to hang over the sides. To make the filling, whisk the eggs and the cream in a bowl and slowly pour onto the marinated pork meat mixture, then add the salt, pepper and nutmeg. Pack the mixture into the terrine and press it down as you do so, with either a spoon or a spatula.

Once the terrine is full, place the thyme on the top and fold the bacon over it, then cover with a lid or a piece of foil. Place the terrine into a deep baking tray and half-fill the tray with hot water, then cook in the oven for 1½ hours, or, if you have a thermometer probe, until the centre reaches 70°C/160°F.

Allow the terrine to cool completely before putting it in the fridge to chill and set. Turn it out to serve.

Serves 4–6

2kg pork mince

30g sea salt

1 heaped tsp ground mace

3 small whole Cox's Orange
   Pippin apples

3 egg yolks

PASTRY:

115g butter

115g lard

50ml milk

a pinch of salt

350g plain flour, plus extra
   for dusting

This may seem like a lot of work, but it's really quite simple, and makes a great centrepiece for any dinner party. It's classically French in shape (you can buy the moulds online, or just use an ordinary one), but it's full of the finest British ingredients.

PORK AND COX'S ORANGE PIPPIN PIE

Put the pork mince in a bowl with the salt and ground mace, then mix well. Set aside in the fridge.

Next, make the pastry. Cut the butter and lard into rough cubes. Bring the butter, lard, milk, 50ml water and salt to the boil in a saucepan, then stir in the flour all at once to form a dough. Remove the pan from the heat and set the dough aside to cool in the fridge for 30 minutes. Lightly flour a work surface and roll out three-quarters of the dough to a 2cm thick round. Line 30cm pork pie mould (or a French-style terrine mould, as shown, or a deep round metal tin) with the pastry. Roll out the rest of the pastry to make a 2cm thick lid.

To assemble the pie, carefully spoon half the pork mixture into the pastry-lined tin, pressing down lightly to ensure there is no trapped air. Place the apples along the centre, then press the remaining pork mixture around them and over the top to cover them completely.

Cover the pie with the pastry lid and seal it all the way around by pinching it together with your index finger and thumb. Poke a small hole in the top of the pie using a sharp knife or skewer. Lightly beat 1 of the egg yolks and brush it over the top of the pie with a pastry brush. Chill the pie in the fridge for 1 hour.

Preheat the oven to 180°C/350°F/Gas mark 4. Brush the pie with a little of the second beaten egg yolk again and bake for 1 hour. Remove the pie from the oven and leave to stand for 5 minutes, then carefully take it out of the mould. Brush with a little more egg yolk around the edges and bake for a further 20 minutes, or until the pastry is crisp.

Remove the pie from the oven and immediately brush it again all over with the final egg yolk. It's important to do this while it's still hot, as this will give it a great colour and shine. Set it aside to cool completely. Chill in the fridge to set before slicing.

Lamb rump should be much more popular than it is. It's the ideal cut of meat for one or two people, almost a mini-joint on its own. It can be simply roasted (it takes about 15 minutes), but I prefer it pot-roasted like this, as you get much more flavour. The cut comes from the top of the leg.

Serves 4

1 red onion

2 large courgettes

1 aubergine

2 red peppers

2 x 300g lamb rumps, off the bone

50ml olive oil

3 garlic cloves

2 large fresh thyme sprigs

125ml white wine

16 Kalamata olives

300ml tomato juice

1 tsp sugar

1 unwaxed lemon

4 fresh basil leaves

sea salt and freshly ground
  black pepper

RUMP OF LAMB WITH PROVENÇAL VEGETABLES

Preheat the oven to 170°C/325°F/Gas mark 3. Cut the onion into 2.5cm dice, the courgettes into 4 large chunks and the aubergine in half lengthways, then each half into 4. Cut the peppers in half, deseed them, then cut the pieces into quarters. Peel the garlic cloves but leave them whole.

Season the lamb with salt and pepper. Place a deep, sturdy roasting pan over a medium heat until hot and add a drizzle of oil. Add the lamb and fry until golden brown on each side, then remove from the pan and set aside. Add the onions, courgettes, aubergines and peppers to the pan and fry for 2–3 minutes. Add the whole garlic cloves, the thyme and the rest of the oil and stir well. Return the lamb to the pan on top of the vegetables and cook in the oven for 1 hour. If it starts to dry out at all, add a splash of water. Once cooked, remove and allow to rest.

Place the pan back over a high heat, add the white wine and bring to the boil, then add the olives and tomato juice. Return to the boil, add the sugar and season with salt and pepper. Grate the lemon zest and tear the basil leaves straight into the pan, then stir well. Remove from the heat, divide the vegetables between the plates, then slice each lamb rump and place the slices on top.

There are two camps when it comes to Irish stew. The purists opt for a less-is-more approach, with just mutton, water, potatoes and onions. Other people will say there should be pearl barley, carrots and other things too. I like to keep it simple: all you need are good-quality meat and vegetables, and the pure flavours don't need anything else.

Serves 4

1.5 litres brown chicken stock

1kg boneless middle neck mutton or lamb

1kg carrots

2 onions

800g all-purpose potatoes

1 large fresh thyme sprig

sea salt and freshly ground black pepper

IRISH STEW

Place a large saucepan or flameproof casserole dish over a medium heat, add the stock and bring to a gentle boil.

Meanwhile, cut the mutton or lamb into 2.5cm cubes and cut the carrots and onions into thick slices. Cut the potatoes into 3–4cm dice. Add the meat to the stock, then reduce the heat until the stock is just simmering. Add the carrots and onions, stir well, then add the potatoes and thyme and cover with a lid.

Simmer for 1½ hours, until the meat is tender and the stock has reduced slightly. Season with salt and pepper and serve.

This is another real chefs' dish – just a plate of this with some frozen peas will do me fine. Lamb mince can sometimes be a bit fatty, so the way I do it is to braise the lamb shoulder separately until tender. You could do this part in advance.

Serves 6–8

1.5kg boneless shoulder of lamb

2 tbsp olive oil

2 large onions

2 garlic cloves

4 carrots

4 fresh rosemary sprigs

300ml red wine

500ml beef stock

sea salt and freshly ground
  black pepper

MASHED POTATOES:

750g floury potatoes

150ml double cream

75g butter

sea salt and freshly ground
  black pepper

SLOW-BRAISED SHEPHERDS' PIE

Preheat the oven to 200°C/400°F/Gas mark 6. Season the lamb shoulder with salt and pepper. Heat a large casserole dish over a medium heat, add the olive oil and the lamb and fry on each side until browned. Finely slice the onions, finely chop the garlic and roughly chop the carrots. Remove the lamb and set aside. Add the onions, garlic and carrots and sweat for 5–10 minutes, until softened.

Return the lamb to the casserole, then add the rosemary and red wine and simmer until reduced by half. Add the beef stock, return to a simmer, then transfer to the oven and cook for 2 hours.

Remove the lamb from the pan and allow it to cool enough to handle. Season the sauce with salt and pepper and set aside. Tear the meat apart using a fork, then place it in the medium casserole with the vegetables and mix it all together.

Meanwhile, cut the potatoes into chunks. Bring a pan of salted water to the boil, add the potatoes and cook for 12–15 minutes, or until tender. Drain well, then return the potatoes to the pan and return to the heat for a few seconds to drive off any excess moisture. Remove the pan from the heat and mash the potatoes until smooth. Add the cream and butter and mash again until smooth, then season with salt and pepper.

Spoon the mashed potatoes over the lamb in the casserole dish. Return to the oven and cook for another 20 minutes, until hot, golden and bubbling.

slow roasts

This recipe is based on one by Thomas Keller of the French Laundry restaurant in Napa Valley, California. I think he's the best chef cooking on the planet. It's great with the Slow-roast Parsnips with Sherry and Chestnuts (page 48).

Serves 4

1 x 1.5kg whole chicken

1 onion

2 carrots

2 tsp flaky sea salt

2 tbsp rapeseed oil

BRINE:

250g flaky sea salt

100g clear honey

8 bay leaves

5 garlic cloves

2 large fresh thyme sprigs

2 lemons

ULTIMATE ROAST CHICKEN

Place all the ingredients for the brine with 5 litres water in a large saucepan, bring to the boil and simmer until the salt and honey have dissolved. Remove from the heat and allow to cool completely. Place the chicken in the cold liquid, then put in the fridge to marinate for about 2 hours.

Preheat the oven to 200°C/400°F/Gas mark 6. Carefully lift the chicken out of the brine (discard the brine), then wash it thoroughly in cold water. Remove the wing tips from the chicken by cutting through the end joint of the wing, then place them in a roasting tin. Roughly chop the onion and carrots, then place them in the tin with the wing tips. Put the chicken on top of them and season it with salt. Drizzle with the rapeseed oil, then roast in the oven for 1 hour.

Turn the chicken around so that it is back to front, then continue cooking for a further 15 minutes. To check if the chicken is cooked, pierce the thickest part of the thigh with a skewer or knife. If the juices run clear, the chicken is cooked. If not, return to the oven for a further 10 minutes, then check again.

Remove the chicken from the oven and allow to rest for 10 minutes before transferring it to a serving plate.

...ing duck slowly is the best way to enjoy the ...le bird, as it ensures that the legs are cooked ...ough properly and the rest is tender. If you cook it slowly, the longer the better. Aylesbury duck is the most popular type, if you can get it.

Serves 4

2 onions

1 leek

2 carrots

1 large duck, ready
  for roasting

a good pinch of sea salt

25g soft butter

1 fresh thyme sprig

400ml chicken stock

100ml port

2 tbsp dark brown sugar

SPICES:

¼ cinnamon stick

1½ tsp coriander seeds

1 tsp cloves

2 juniper berries

1 bay leaf

1 tbsp black peppercorns

1½ tsp sea salt

ROAST DUCK WITH PORT AND WINTER SPICES

Preheat the oven to 170°C/325°F/Gas mark 3. Cut the onions into quarters and roughly chop the leek and carrots. Place all the spices and salt in a spice grinder or pestle and mortar and grind to a fine powder.

Pierce the skin of the duck with a large fork – this allows the fat to escape – then rub it with the butter. Season with salt and sprinkle with half of the spice mixture. Place the vegetables, thyme, chicken stock, port and sugar in a roasting tin, then put the duck on top of the vegetables (this prevents the duck from browning too much on the bottom). Cover with foil and cook in the oven for about 1½ hours, basting occasionally with the juices.

Remove the foil and return to the oven for another 30 minutes. When the duck is cooked, remove it from the tin, sprinkle with the remaining spice mixture and allow to rest for 10 minutes. Carve it into thick slices before serving with the pan juices.

For me, this is the best recipe in the book. Who doesn't love pork crackling? The great thing about using shoulder is that the fat will make the skin crispy and stop the meat from becoming dry, so you get the best of both worlds. The longer it's cooked for, the better it is. It's near impossible to carve – just place it in the centre of the table and dive in. The scrumpy works a treat with it.

Serves 6–8

3.5kg boned pork shoulder, in one piece

4 tbsp olive oil

15g sea salt

2 Bramley apples

80g butter

75ml scrumpy cider

2–4 tbsp caster sugar

1 pointed (sweetheart) cabbage

sea salt and freshly ground black pepper

SLOW-ROAST PORK SHOULDER WITH SCRUMPY AND APPLE SAUCE

Preheat the oven to 240°C/475°F/Gas mark 9. Score the skin of the pork with a sharp knife into strips, then rub the surface with the olive oil and sea salt. Place in a deep-sided roasting tin with 500ml water and cook in the oven, uncovered, for 40 minutes. This will help set the crackling. Cover with foil, reduce the temperature to 150°C/300°F/Gas mark 2 and cook for 3½ hours, until very tender and golden brown.

Remove the pork from the oven and allow to rest for 30 minutes. Peel and chop the apples and put them in a saucepan with 50g of the butter and the scrumpy. Cover and place over a medium heat. Cook gently for about 4–5 minutes, until the apples have broken down. Stir and season with the sugar and a little salt.

Shred the cabbage. Heat a frying pan until hot and add the remaining butter, cabbage and 75ml water. Cook until just tender, then season with salt and pepper. Slice or shred the meat from the pork shoulder with a fork and pile it onto a serving plate with some of the pan juices, the cabbage and a large dollop of apple sauce.

Henry VIII would be proud of this dish. Sure, it's not a huge pig like the ones he ate, but the smaller ones can be ordered from your butcher. I was a pig farmer in my youth and we ate this kind of food a lot. Food like this should be back on our tables more often: it's a real celebration dish, and I think that sometimes we don't celebrate food enough.

Serves 8–10

1 x 8kg whole suckling pig
4 large carrots
4 parsnips

3–4 tbsp rapeseed oil
100g English mustard
sea salt and freshly ground
　black pepper

ROAST SUCKLING PIG WITH ENGLISH MUSTARD

Preheat the oven to 170°C/325°F/Gas mark 3. Ensure the cavity and the skin of the pig is thoroughly cleaned and rinsed, then pat dry with kitchen paper and season the pig with sea salt. Place the carrots and parsnips, whole, in a roasting tin, season with salt and pepper and put the pig on top. Drizzle with some rapeseed oil and pour 300ml water into the tin. Cover with greaseproof paper along the back of the pig, cover the whole tin with foil, then roast in the oven for about 1½ hours.

Remove the pork from the oven and increase the temperature to 180°C/350°F/Gas mark 4. Remove the foil and greaseproof paper, stir the vegetables around and return the pig to the oven to cook for 1 hour more. Remove and allow to rest for at least 15 minutes. Carve into thick slices and serve with English mustard and the roasted carrots and parsnips.

Serves 4

RIBS:

2kg individual, meaty pork ribs

6 garlic cloves

a 10cm piece of fresh ginger

6 spring onions

2 tbsp vegetable oil

1 tsp dried chilli flakes

2 tsp Chinese five-spice powder

1 tsp ground cinnamon

650ml chicken stock

250ml rice wine or dry sherry

200ml soy sauce

150g demerara sugar

4 tbsp sesame oil

grated zest of 2 unwaxed oranges

CABBAGE SLAW:

800g red cabbage

1 red onion

3 red chillies

150ml white wine vinegar

50g caster sugar

100ml coconut milk

4 tbsp fresh coriander leaves

4 tbsp fresh mint leaves

sea salt and freshly ground
     black pepper

Chinese cooks really know how to use the lesser-known cuts of meat, so no slow-cooking collection could be without a few of their techniques and flavours. This recipe is great: just put the ribs in the oven and they become lovely and sticky as they cook. Serving it with slaw is more American than Chinese, but they work so well together.

CHINESE-SPICED PORK RIBS WITH CABBAGE SLAW

Preheat the oven to 140°C/275°F/Gas mark 1. Place the ribs in a large roasting tin. Finely chop the garlic and ginger and roughly chop the spring onions. Heat a frying pan until hot, add the vegetable oil and heat until smoking, then add the garlic, ginger and spring onions and stir-fry quickly for 30 seconds. Add the spices and fry for another few seconds, then add the stock, rice wine or sherry, soy sauce and sugar and bring to a simmer. Cook for a couple of minutes until the sugar has dissolved, then add the sesame oil and orange zest and stir to combine. Pour the mixture straight over the ribs and toss so that everything is coated in the sauce. Cover with foil and cook in the oven for 2¼ hours.

Meanwhile, deseed the chillies, then slice the red cabbage, onion and chillies as thinly as you can. Heat the vinegar, sugar and coconut milk in a pan until simmering. Once the sugar has melted, put the red cabbage mixture in a bowl and pour the hot vinegar mixture over the top, stirring well. Leave to steep for at least 15 minutes, then add the rest of the slaw ingredients, season with salt and pepper, and mix well.

Remove the foil and turn the ribs over in the sauce until they are well glazed, then return to the oven, uncovered, for another 45 minutes, until just sticky – you might want to turn them again during this time. Remove the ribs from the oven and allow to rest for 5 minutes before serving. Turn them once more in the glaze before serving. Pile them onto a serving platter with a bowl of the cabbage alongside, and dig in.

How good do these look? In the restaurant we serve them on a board with a bowl of mixed leaves and some home-made mustard. It's a dish that takes time to cook, but, like most things in this book, while it's cooking you don't need to worry about it. Ham hocks are sometimes known as pork or gammon knuckles. If you've got a good butcher nearby, they'll be able to get them for you.

Serves 4

2 carrots
1 large onion
3 tbsp cloves
4 x 500g ham hocks
1 celery stick

3 fresh flat-leaf parsley sprigs
1 fresh thyme sprig
1 bay leaf
a pinch of sea salt
125g black treacle
2 heads Little Gem lettuce

TREACLE-GLAZED HAM HOCKS

Cut the carrots in half lengthways and stud the onion with 2 of the cloves. Place the ham hocks in a deep saucepan, add the onion, carrots, celery and herbs, cover with cold water and add a pinch of salt. Bring slowly to the boil over a medium-low heat, then gently simmer for 2 hours. Turn off the heat and allow to cool slightly.

Preheat the oven to 200°C/400°F/Gas mark 6. Carefully remove the ham hocks from the liquid and place them in a roasting tin. Using a sharp knife, remove the skin and trim off any excess fat to reveal the pink meat underneath, then insert cloves at regular intervals over each hock. Return the hocks to the oven for 10 minutes to dry the surface of the meat.

Meanwhile, gently warm the black treacle in a saucepan. After 10 minutes, remove the hocks from the oven, spoon over the treacle and return to the oven for a further 20–30 minutes, basting occasionally.

Separate out the leaves of the lettuce. Once the hocks are shiny and glazed, remove from the oven and serve with the lettuce leaves and a dollop of wholegrain mustard.

This recipe is a twist on a dish I ate in India. They cooked it on charcoal there, but it's far easier to do it in the oven. The flavour of guinea fowl is somewhere between that of pheasant and chicken, and it's a great meat for people who aren't too fond of game but want to try something new.

Serves 4

MARINADE:

200ml yoghurt

1 tbsp crushed fresh ginger

1 tbsp crushed garlic

½ tsp turmeric

2 tsp ground coriander

½ tsp ground cinnamon

1 tsp ground cumin

1 tsp red chilli powder

¼ tsp ground fenugreek

½ tsp garam masala

1 tbsp lemon juice

2 guinea fowls, cleaned

PILAU RICE:

1 onion

a 5cm piece of fresh ginger

2 garlic cloves

3 green cardamom pods, split

½ tsp ground coriander

½ tsp ground cumin

1 tsp sea salt

8 curry leaves

400g basmati rice

3 tbsp fresh coriander leaves

juice of ½ lemon

INDIAN-SPICED GUINEA FOWL WITH PILAU RICE

Put all the marinade ingredients in a bowl and stir well. Add the guinea fowl and coat well, massaging the marinade into the meat. Cover with clingfilm and leave in the fridge for 1 hour, or preferably overnight, to marinate.

Preheat the oven to 150°C/300°F/Gas mark 2. Finely dice the onion, ginger and garlic and place in a 20 x 30 x 4cm roasting tin. Add the spices and rice and stir well. Add 600ml water and stir to combine, making sure there are no clumps of rice.

Place the marinated guinea fowl on top of the rice, making sure they are well spaced out. Cover with foil, then cook in the oven for 45 minutes. Remove the foil, then return to the oven for another 15 minutes to brown and finish cooking through.

Remove from the oven and leave to rest for 5 minutes. Meanwhile, chop the coriander and sprinkle it and the lemon juice over the guinea fowl and rice. Serve immediately and carve it at the table.

Unlike most birds, goose breasts can be served pink if you roast them separately, but as a whole bird it's better to slow-roast it. Always use some form of trivet to lift the goose away from the large amount of fat that will come out during cooking. I've used vegetables for that here. My mother used to cook hers in the Aga overnight and it tasted even better. Use the 3 hours suggested here as a guide; you can cook it for a lot longer if you like, for up to 5 hours at 170°C/325°F/Gas mark 3.

Serves 4

2 onions

2 carrots

2 celery sticks

8 fresh thyme sprigs

1 tbsp pink peppercorns

1 tsp salt

4 tbsp honey

4 tbsp extra-virgin olive oil

1 x 4.5kg goose, cleaned

200ml white wine

350ml chicken stock

sea salt and freshly ground
  black pepper

SLOW-ROAST GOOSE WITH THYME AND HONEY

Preheat the oven to 220°C/450°F/Gas mark 7. Cut the onions, carrots and celery into large chunks and place them in a deep-sided roasting tin. Put the thyme, peppercorns and salt into a pestle and mortar and grind to a rough paste. Add the honey and olive oil and mix well.

Place the goose on top of the vegetables, then spread the honey mixture all over it, rubbing well into the skin. Roast in the oven for 30 minutes, then reduce the temperature to 180°C/350°F/Gas mark 4 and roast for another 2½ hours, basting with the juices every so often. Remove from the oven and carefully lift the goose out onto a serving platter, then cover with foil and allow to rest for 30 minutes. Skim off as much of the fat as you can – you can reserve this for roasting potatoes.

Place the tin over a medium heat until the juices are bubbling, then add the wine and deglaze, stirring up all the sediment on the bottom of the tin. Add the chicken stock and bring to a simmer, cook for 5 minutes, then season with salt and pepper. Strain through a sieve into a sauce boat and serve with the goose. Potatoes roasted in the goose fat would be delicious with this.

There's a lot of flavour in hay, and this style of cooking can work with chicken and venison as well as lamb. Using the hay is all about adding flavour, and you could even include a bit of lavender if you like. You need to get your fresh hay from a pet shop, not from the local farmer who sells it as bedding for horses. It's good with Potato and Turnip Dauphinoise (page 42).

Serves 6–8

1 whole garlic bulb

1 x 2.7kg whole leg of lamb

3 tbsp rapeseed oil

about ½ bag eating hay from
  a pet shop

sea salt and freshly ground
  black pepper

ROAST LEG OF LAMB IN HAY

Preheat the oven to 180°C/350°F/Gas mark 4. Separate, peel and slice the garlic cloves lengthways. Using a sharp knife, prick the leg of lamb about 20 times all over, about 2cm deep, then place a slice of garlic into each hole. Drizzle with oil, season well with salt and pepper and set aside.

Place a large roasting tin or flameproof casserole dish over a medium heat, and when it is hot place the hay in the bottom. When the hay starts to smoke a little, place the lamb leg in the middle. The hay should come half way up the lamb. Cover it with a lid or foil. Transfer straight to the oven and cook for 2 hours, then remove the lid or foil, increase the temperature to 200°C/400°F/Gas mark 6 and cook for another 30 minutes.

Remove the lamb from the oven and allow to cool for 10 minutes. Carefully lift it out of the tin and brush off the hay. Slice and serve with mint jelly.

Lamb belly is great to stuff and roll – you buy it in a long piece and it is nice and flat, allowing you to roll it easily. Cooking it slowly makes the meat nice and tender. The leftovers are great cold served with salad, too.

Serves 4

1 boneless lamb belly

1 onion

2 garlic cloves

tops of 3 green leeks

1 tbsp olive oil

200g dried breadcrumbs

75g soft butter, plus extra
  for greasing

sea salt and freshly ground
  black pepper

HERB CRUMBS:

50g fresh flat-leaf parsley leaves

25g fresh chives

1 fresh rosemary sprig

200g dried breadcrumbs

LEEK-STUFFED BELLY OF LAMB WITH HERB CRUMBS

Preheat the oven to 170°C/325°F/Gas mark 3. Grease a large piece of foil, put the lamb belly on it, skin-side down, and season with salt and pepper.

Finely chop the onion and garlic. Cut the leek tops into 1cm dice and wash them thoroughly. Place a pan over a medium heat, add the olive oil, onion and garlic and cook until just softened. Add the leek tops and sweat for another minute, then remove and set aside.

Place the breadcrumbs, leek mixture and soft butter into a bowl, mix well and season with salt and pepper. Spread the breadcrumb mixture over the lamb belly, then roll it up into a Swiss roll shape, starting from the long side. Wrap the foil around it tightly to form a large sausage, and twist the ends of the foil to seal. Roast in the oven for 1½ hours.

Remove from the oven and take off the foil, reserving any cooking juices, then return it to the oven to continue cooking for a further 15 minutes.

Meanwhile, place the parsley, chives, rosemary and breadcrumbs into a food processor and process until the mixture turns green and forms a fine powder, then remove and transfer to a tray. Remove the lamb from the oven and allow to rest for 20 minutes, spooning over some of the reserved cooking juices. Roll the lamb through the green breadcrumbs, then place on a serving dish and serve.

I first came across this cooking method a few years ago, and at first I wasn't too sure. To me, cooking food wrapped in plastic isn't proper cooking. But this dish really works: you don't need any fancy equipment, just time and a low oven. There are complicated explanations, but, being a Yorkshireman, I like to keep things simple. Basically, long, low-temperature cooking means that the fibres in the meat don't firm up too much. It's a bit like when you tense up on getting into a hot bath — when you get in a warm bath, you don't, and that's why this beef tastes so good. Before you start, check that your clingfilm is suitable for use with all foods and at 80°C (175°F).

Serves 4–6

2 tbsp vegetable oil

1.5kg well hung, middle-cut fillet
  of beef

50g butter

sea salt and freshly ground
  black pepper

SLOW-COOKED BEEF FILLET

Preheat the oven to 80°C/175°F/Gas Mark ¼. Heat a frying pan over a medium heat until it is hot, then add a tablespoon of the oil. Place the beef in the pan and fry it briefly, turning it occasionally, until browned on all sides — no more than 2 minutes in total. Remove from the pan and allow to cool.

Lay out some clingfilm on a clean, dry work surface: you need 4 large rectangles that completely overlap. Place the beef along the long edge of the clingfilm and roll it up tightly, holding both ends so it forms a large cylindrical Christmas cracker shape. Tie a knot in each end and place in a roasting tin. Cook in the oven for 1 hour. Remove the beef from the oven and remove and discard the clingfilm.

Heat a frying pan until hot, then add the remaining oil and the butter. When it's foaming, add the beef. Turn the fillet until evenly browned — no more than 30 seconds on each side. Remove the fillet from the pan, place it on a carving board and allow to rest for 5 minutes. Slice it thickly and season with salt and pepper, then serve with wholegrain mustard.

There are lots of blackberry bushes near where I live, and I always go and pick them to turn into jam or use in cooking. The big, prize juicy ones are at the top – I always avoid the berries lower down the bush.

Serves 6

1 carrot

1 red onion

1 tbsp rapeseed oil

1 x 2.5kg haunch of venison, on the bone

1 fresh thyme sprig

6 juniper berries

2 bay leaves

300g blackberries

SAUCE:

125ml red wine

300ml beef stock

25g butter

sea salt and freshly ground black pepper

ROAST HAUNCH OF VENISON WITH BLACKBERRIES

Preheat the oven to 170°C/325°F/Gas mark 3. Cut the carrot in half lengthways, then roughly chop the red onion. Heat a non-stick pan over a medium heat, then add the rapeseed oil and venison. Cook on each side until browned, then set aside.

Put the carrot, onion, thyme, juniper berries and bay leaves into a heavy roasting tin, then place the venison on top. Roast in the oven for 1¼ hours.

Meanwhile, crush half the blackberries in a bowl with the back of a fork, then spoon them over the haunch. Return to the oven for a further 15 minutes.

Remove the venison from the oven, take it out of the roasting tin and set aside to rest on a chopping board. Strain the cooking juices into a bowl, discarding the vegetables and juniper berries. Place the tin over a medium heat and add the red wine, stirring up all the sediment on the bottom of the pan. Add the beef stock and reserved cooking juices and bring to the boil. Add the rest of the blackberries, return to the boil, then whisk in the butter. Remove from the heat, season with salt and pepper and pour into a gravy boat. Slice the venison and serve.

slow stews & braises

The word 'confit' refers to the method of cooking meats such as chicken, pork, goose or duck in their own fat and keeping them covered in the same fat to prevent them from coming into contact with the air. It has been used as a method of preserving meat for hundreds of years, and the same technique is used in many restaurants today. They may use water baths, plastic bags and digital thermometers, but the process is still the same. I believe there are few chefs, even those with two or three Michelin stars, who can cook a confit of duck better than a French grandmother using a cassoulet dish. That's proper food.

Serves 4

4 duck legs

15g salt per kg of duck legs

2–3 fresh thyme sprigs

500g duck fat

4 tbsp clear honey

CLASSIC DUCK CONFIT

First, weigh the duck legs. This is the most important part, as doing so will tell you how much salt is needed to cure them. Once weighed, put them in a roasting tin. Pick the leaves from the thyme and sprinkle the duck with 15g salt per kilogram of duck, and the thyme leaves. Wrap with clingfilm and place in the fridge overnight, or for at least 12 hours.

The next day, remove the duck from the tin, rinse off the salt and dry with a clean tea towel. Place in a large pan, add the duck fat and cook slowly at a very gentle simmer in the fat for about 1½ hours – you will see that the meat has shrunk away from the bone. Do not allow the fat to boil. Once cooked, turn off the heat and allow the duck to cool in the fat. At this point it can be kept in the fridge, covered with fat, for up to 1 week.

Preheat the oven to 200°C/400°F/Gas mark 6. Scrape the fat off the duck legs and place in a roasting tin. Smear the honey over the duck. Roast the legs in the oven for about 20 minutes, spooning the honey glaze over them 2 or 3 times, then serve. It's great with cooked green French beans or buttered mashed potatoes.

Pheasants usually come in braces (pairs), and the cock pheasant is larger than the hen once all the feathers have been removed, but when pot-roasting them like this the size doesn't really matter. Game birds are usually either roasted quickly or cooked long and slow. The advantage of the long, slow method is that you can eat the lot – quick cooking often means you have to throw away the carcass and legs, and just use the breast meat.

Serves 4

4 cloves

1 cinnamon stick

2 star anise pods

½ tsp mixed spice

2 carrots

1 onion

1 celery stick

2 garlic cloves

3–4 tbsp rapeseed oil

2 pheasants, cleaned and
  giblets removed

400ml Riesling wine

550ml chicken stock

sea salt and freshly ground
  black pepper

BRAISED PHEASANT WITH CINNAMON AND STAR ANISE

Heat a frying pan until hot, add the cloves, cinnamon, star anise and mixed spice, and toast them lightly. Tip into a spice grinder or pestle and mortar and process to a fine powder.

Preheat the oven to 200°C/400°F/Gas mark 6. Roughly chop the carrots, onion and celery and crush the garlic. Heat a flameproof casserole dish over a medium heat, ensuring it is large enough to hold the 2 pheasants with a lid. Drizzle in a little of the oil and fry the pheasants one at a time, turning them, until evenly golden brown all over. Remove and set aside.

Return the casserole to the heat, add a little more oil, add the vegetables and garlic and cook for 3–4 minutes. Return the pheasants to the casserole and add the white wine. Bring to a simmer, then cook until reduced by half. Add the stock, return to the boil, then reduce to a simmer and sprinkle the pheasant with the spice powder and season with salt and pepper. Cover with the lid and cook in the oven for 1 hour.

Remove the lid and return to the oven for 15 minutes, to allow the skin to crisp up. Remove from the oven and serve with buttery mashed potatoes.

Harissa is a chilli paste or sauce often used in North African cooking. Made mainly from chillies, it also contains caraway, garlic and oil, and can be used to flavour dishes like this one, or couscous.

Serves 4

STEW:

1 whole chicken, jointed into
  8 pieces, or 8 chicken thighs

2 onions

3 garlic cloves

4 potatoes

2 pickled lemons

800ml chicken stock

2 tbsp olive oil

4 tbsp fresh coriander leaves

250g Greek yoghurt

sea salt and freshly ground
  black pepper

HARISSA:

25g dried red chillies

3 fresh red chillies

1 tbsp ground cumin

1 tsp ground caraway seeds

1 tbsp hot smoked paprika

4 garlic cloves

4 tbsp olive oil

HARISSA CHICKEN AND POTATO STEW

To make the harissa, put the dried chillies in a bowl and just cover with water, then soak for 20 minutes. Deseed and roughly chop the fresh chillies. Strain the soaked chillies (reserving the water), discard the stalks and roughly chop them. Put them in a food processor or pestle and mortar with the rest of the harissa ingredients. Process or pound until puréed, then add some of the reserved water and continue processing to form a smooth paste. Put the chicken in a bowl with half the harissa paste and stir well. Put it in the fridge to marinate for at least 4 hours, or preferably overnight.

Thickly slice the onions and garlic. Cut the potatoes into medium chunks. Cut the pickled lemons into thick slices. Heat a large flameproof casserole dish, add half the olive oil and half the chicken and fry on each side until browned. Remove, set aside and repeat with the rest of the chicken.

Add the onions and garlic to the pan and cook until softened with a little colour. Add the rest of the harissa paste and cook for 1 minute, then return the chicken to the pan. Add the potatoes, pickled lemons and chicken stock. Bring to the boil, then reduce the heat and simmer for 1¼ hours over a very gentle heat, until cooked through and slightly thickened. Meanwhile, roughly chop the coriander. Season the stew with salt and pepper, then whisk in the yoghurt and stir in the coriander.

I think I was in my teens when I first cooked lamb shanks, and back then they only cost a few pence each. They're getting more expensive as more people cook them, but they're worth it – the flavours from the long, slow cooking make it a great cut of meat to use. You can also cook them in a slow cooker on a low setting for 12 hours.

Serves 4

50g plain flour

4 lamb shanks

2 tbsp olive oil

300g baby onions or shallots

400ml good red wine

300ml chicken or beef stock

2 bay leaves

4 fresh rosemary sprigs

40g butter

3 tbsp fresh flat-leaf parsley leaves

sea salt and freshly ground
 black pepper

LAMB SHANKS BRAISED IN RED WINE

Preheat the oven to 150°C/300°F/Gas mark 2. Season the flour with salt and black pepper, then dust the lamb shanks with the flour, shaking off any excess. Heat a large, heavy-based, ovenproof pan until hot, then add the olive oil and fry the lamb for 4–5 minutes, until well browned on each side. This will help give the dish a nice brown colour once cooked.

Meanwhile, peel the baby onions or shallots and leave them whole. The best way to do this is to place them in a heatproof bowl, pour over a kettleful of boiling water, leave to stand for a few minutes, then drain them. Once cooled, the skins will slip off more easily.

Add the onions to the pan with the lamb and cook until browned, then add the red wine and stir to release any sediment on the bottom of the pan. Add the stock and bring to a simmer, then add the bay leaves and rosemary. Cover with foil or a lid and cook slowly in the oven for 6–8 hours, basting occasionally.

Remove from the oven, carefully remove the shanks from the pan and place in a serving dish. Cut the butter into cubes and chop the parsley. Taste and season the sauce with salt and pepper, then whisk in the butter gradually, and stir in the chopped parsley. Serve the lamb shanks with buttery mashed potatoes, with the sauce over the top.

Serves 4

RAS-EL-HANOUT:

10 cardamom pods

1 tsp whole cloves

1 tsp ground cinnamon

1 tsp ground cumin

1 tsp coriander seeds

1 tsp fenugreek seeds

1 tsp fennel seeds

1 tsp mustard seeds

1 tsp hot smoked paprika

1 tsp turmeric

10g dried rose petals

1 tsp sea salt

LAMB:

1kg diced leg of lamb

2 red onions

vegetable oil, for frying

3 garlic cloves

a 5cm piece of fresh ginger

2 red chillies

1 litre chicken stock

250g stoned prunes

2 tbsp honey

10g fresh mint or coriander leaves

TABBOULEH:

175g bulghur wheat

700ml chicken stock

2 small red onions

100g pistachio nuts

100g toasted hazelnuts

100g toasted walnuts

5 tbsp fresh mint leaves

juice of 1 lemon

3 tbsp extra-virgin olive oil

5 tbsp fresh flat-leaf parsley leaves

sea salt and freshly ground
  black pepper

Ras-el-hanout translates roughly to 'top of the shop' and is a Moroccan spice mixture that can be found in most supermarkets. It's usually a mixture of chilli, coriander, cumin, turmeric and peppercorns, but some contain as many as 100 different spices. Its name means that you should get a mixture of the best spices the seller has to offer.

LAMB RAS-EL-HANOUT WITH NUT TABBOULEH

Remove the cardamom seeds from the pods and place all the ras-el-hanout ingredients in a spice grinder, then pulse to form a powder. Remove and set aside. Put the lamb in a large bowl, sprinkle over 3 tablespoons of the spice mixture and toss through the meat, ensuring it is well coated. Leave to marinate for 20 minutes. Reserve the rest of the spice mix for use later.

Preheat the oven to 170°C/325°F/Gas mark 3. Cut the red onions into 2.5cm dice. Finely chop the garlic, ginger and chillies. Put a flameproof casserole dish over a medium heat and add a little vegetable oil. Add the lamb and cook in batches until golden brown, then remove from the pan. Increase the heat, add the red onions and fry until golden brown. Add the garlic, ginger and chillies and fry for 1 minute. Add the rest of the spice mixture and fry for a further minute. Return the lamb to the pan, add the stock, bring to the boil and add the prunes. Cover with a lid and cook in the oven for 1 hour. Remove the lid and continue to cook for a further 30 minutes, until thickened, then remove from the oven. Taste and season with salt and pepper if necessary.

Meanwhile, make the tabbouleh. Put the bulghur wheat in a saucepan with the chicken stock and bring to the boil, then reduce the heat to a simmer. Cover and cook for 15–20 minutes over a very low heat, until all the liquid is absorbed and the wheat is tender. Meanwhile, finely chop the red onions, then roughly chop the nuts and herbs.

Allow the bulghur wheat to cool slightly before placing in a bowl with the red onions, pistachios, hazelnuts, walnuts nuts, lemon juice, olive oil and herbs. Stir well until thoroughly mixed, then season with salt and pepper. Chop the fresh mint or coriander leaves and scatter them over the lamb. Serve the lamb with the tabbouleh.

You can confit most meats – classically, it's done with duck legs. It's a great way of using cheaper cuts and making them tender. The secret is not to let the oil or fat boil: the idea is to cook the meat at around 80°C (175°F), so a gentle bubbling is what you need. Accompaniments such as gherkins and capers are great with it because they cut through the fat.

Serves 4

1kg lamb neck fillet, fully trimmed

1–2 litres rapeseed oil

3 heads Little Gem lettuce

2 banana shallots

75g gherkins

3 tbsp fresh flat-leaf parsley leaves

3 tbsp fresh mint leaves

75g capers, drained

3 tbsp extra-virgin olive oil

sea salt and freshly ground
  black pepper

CONFIT LAMB SALAD WITH CAPERS AND GHERKINS

Put the lamb in a large sauté pan or deep frying pan, making sure the pan is big enough to hold it all in one layer, then pour over enough rapeseed oil to completely cover the lamb. Place over a medium-low heat and bring to a very gentle simmer, just enough for a few tiny bubbles to burst on the surface. Simmer at that temperature for 1¼ hours, or until the lamb is tender.

When the lamb has cooked, allow it to cool in the oil for 30 minutes, then lift it out and place on kitchen paper to drain and cool.

Meanwhile, separate the Little Gem leaves and thinly slice the shallots and gherkins. Roughly chop the parsley and mint leaves. When the lamb is cool enough to handle, shred it into large pieces. Layer the lettuce with the shredded lamb, shallots, capers, gherkins, parsley and mint. Season with a little salt and pepper, then drizzle with the olive oil.

1 onion

1 carrot

1 celery stick

1 leek

½ head garlic

4 fresh thyme sprigs

2 fresh rosemary sprigs

2 star anise pods

3 whole black peppercorns

2 cinnamon sticks

1 x 1.5kg lamb belly, bones removed

150ml chilli sauce

SALAD:

1 white turnip

1 cucumber

110ml white wine vinegar

1 tsp sugar

1 tsp salt

4 tbsp fresh mint leaves

4 tbsp fresh coriander leaves

150g watercress leaves

1 punnet salad or coriander
  cress (optional)

This dish is well worth trying. It's so simple once the meat is cooked, as all you do is slice it and pan-fry it to warm it up. The pickled turnip and cucumber make it really light and fresh tasting. Belly of lamb isn't used very often, but it's a great cut of meat, and economical too.

LAMB RASHERS WITH PICKLED TURNIP AND CUCUMBER

Preheat the oven to 150°C/300°F/Gas mark 2. Roughly chop the onion, carrot, celery, leek and garlic and place in a deep-sided roasting tin with the herbs and spices. Place the lamb on top, then pour over 1.5 litres water. Cover with foil and put in the oven to poach for 2 hours.

Meanwhile, make the salad. Thinly slice the turnip and cucumber, using a mandoline if you have one. Put them in a heatproof bowl. Put 110ml water in a pan with the white wine vinegar, sugar and salt, and heat until the salt and sugar have dissolved. Pour over the turnip and cucumber and set aside to pickle for 2 hours, then drain off the pickling liquid.

Remove the lamb from the oven and allow to cool completely – in the fridge is best. Remove it from the cooking liquid, slice it into 1.5cm thick slices. When ready to serve, heat a large non-stick frying pan and fry the lamb slices on both sides over a high heat, until they are nicely browned and have a caramelized colour. Add a few tablespoons of the chilli sauce to the pan – this will help with the colouring.

Transfer the lamb to serving plates and add the slices of pickled turnip and cucumber, watercress leaves, then the coriander and mint, and salad or coriander cress, if using. Drizzle over the remaining chilli sauce, and serve.

Serves 4

16 pork cheeks, trimmed

1 onion

2 carrots

2 garlic cloves

2 tbsp olive oil

2 fresh thyme sprigs

2 bay leaves

500ml good white wine

200ml chicken stock

sea salt and freshly ground
black pepper

BUTCHERS' SAUCE:

2 onions

75g butter

2 large gherkins

3 tbsp fresh flat-leaf parsley leaves

125ml white wine

250ml brown chicken stock

1 tbsp English mustard

This type of dish is appearing more and more often on restaurant menus, which surprised me a little at first. But I love pork cheeks: it's the part of the animal that does the most work, and so in my mind has the best flavour. They're cheap too, and easy to get hold of from your butcher. Ask for the membrane to be removed, though, as they can sometimes be tough if you leave it on, even if you cook them for a long time.

BRAISED PORK CHEEKS WITH BUTCHERS' SAUCE

Preheat the oven to 150°C/300°F/Gas mark 2. Season the pork cheeks with salt and pepper. Thickly slice the onion, carrots and garlic. Heat a large flameproof casserole dish until hot, add the olive oil and pork cheeks in batches, and fry on each side until golden brown. Remove from the pan and set aside.

Add the onions, carrots and garlic to the pan and cook over a medium heat until softened, then return the pork cheeks to the pan and add the herbs and white wine. Bring to the boil, then cook until reduced by half. Add the chicken stock and bring to a simmer. Cook in the oven for 2 hours, until the cheeks are tender. Strain off the cooking liquid – you won't need it for this dish, but it would be great as the base of a soup.

Meanwhile, make the butchers' sauce. Finely slice the onions. Heat a large frying pan until hot, add the butter and sliced onions and cook over a medium heat for 30 minutes, stirring frequently, until very soft and golden brown. Cut the gherkins into thin strips and roughly chop the parsley.

Increase the heat slightly, then add the wine and stir well into the onions, picking up any sediment on the bottom of the pan. Cook until nearly evaporated. Cut the butter into cubes. Add the stock and bring to a simmer, cook for 5 minutes, then gradually whisk in the butter and cook until just thickened and glossy. Stir in the English mustard, gherkins and the parsley and season with salt and pepper. Spoon over the pork cheeks and serve with mashed potatoes.

Serves 4–6

2kg boneless beef shin or
   featherblade, in large chunks

2 tsp black peppercorns

3 tbsp flour

1.5 litres full-bodied red wine

9 garlic cloves

1 bouquet garni

3 large carrots

3 shallots

2 tbsp fresh flat leaf-parsley

olive oil, for frying

300ml beef stock

25g butter

sea salt and freshly ground
   black pepper

MUSTARD MASH:

750g floury potatoes

150ml double cream

75g butter

2 tbsp wholegrain mustard

Featherblade is cut of meat you don't often see in the supermarkets, as it tends to be used for pies and mince, but ask your butcher to get it for you. It can also be braised with red wine and shallots, a bit like a coq au vin – delicious.

BRAISED FEATHERBLADE OF BEEF WITH MUSTARD MASH

Put the beef in a deep roasting tin and season with salt and pepper. Crush the peppercorns. Mix the flour, wine, garlic, peppercorns and bouquet garni together and pour over the beef. Cover with clingfilm and marinate in the fridge for 12 hours.

Preheat the oven to 170°C/325°F/Gas mark 3. Remove the beef from the fridge, discard the clingfilm and cover the roasting tin with foil. Cook in the oven for 3 hours, or until the meat is so tender it flakes when pressed with the back of a spoon. Leave to cool in the tray.

Meanwhile, finely dice the carrot, finely chop the shallots and roughly chop the parsley. Heat a little oil in a sauté pan and cook the shallots and carrots gently for 2 minutes, until softened. Leave to cool. Lift the meat out of the tray and flake it, discarding any sinew or excess fat, into a bowl. Pass the cooking liquor through a fine sieve into a bowl, reserve 300ml and discard the rest. Add the carrot, shallots and parsley to the meat along with the reserved cooking liquor and mix well, then season with salt and pepper.

Put 4 large pieces of clingfilm on top of each other on a clean work surface. Spoon the meat in a line onto it, then roll it up to form a sausage shape. Tie the ends tightly and put in the fridge for about 40 minutes to firm up.

Put the stock in a saucepan and simmer until reduced by half and slightly thickened. Meanwhile, make the mash. Boil the potatoes in a pan of salted water for 12–15 minutes, until tender. Drain well, then return to the pan and put back on the heat briefly to drive off any excess moisture. Remove from the heat and mash the potatoes until smooth. Add the cream, butter and mustard and mash again until smooth, then season with salt and pepper.

Remove the beef from the fridge and cut it into 5cm discs, then take off the clingfilm. Heat a non-stick frying pan over a medium heat, add the beef and cook until browned on each side. Increase the heat slightly, add the butter and cook for 4–5 minutes, spooning it over the beef. Be careful not to break up the meat. To serve, put the mash in a serving bowl, place the beef on top and spoon the beef stock over the beef.

Serves 4

SPICE PASTE:

150g shallots

a 3cm piece of fresh galangal

3 lemongrass stalks

5 garlic cloves

a 3cm piece of fresh ginger

1–2 tbsp crushed dried chillies,
    according to taste

BEEF:

1kg beef shin, boned

5 tbsp vegetable oil

2 cinnamon sticks

3 cloves

3 star anise pods

3 cardamom pods

1 lemongrass stalk

6 tbsp toasted desiccated coconut

400ml coconut milk

2 tbsp tamarind paste

1 tbsp fish sauce

1 tbsp soy sauce

6 kaffir lime leaves

250ml beef stock

juice of 1 lime

sea salt and freshly ground
    black pepper

COCONUT RICE:

250g basmati rice

150ml coconut milk

Rendang is originally from Indonesia, but it's now popular all over southeast Asia, and I tried it most recently in Singapore. Although many people think it's a curry, a traditional rendang is really nothing like a curry, but – as with so many dishes – it has been adapted to suit people's tastes over the years. It is tradionally made with beef, but you can also use chicken, liver, mutton or duck. Add as much chilli to the spice paste as you dare.

BEEF RENDANG

To make the spice paste, roughly chop the shallots, galangal, lemongrass, garlic and ginger, then place all the ingredients into a food processor and pulse, adding as much water as necessary (about 4–5 tablespoons) to make a fine paste. Remove and set aside.

Cut the beef into 4cm cubes. Heat a heavy-based pan over a medium heat, add half the oil and the beef, in batches if necessary, and cook on all sides until browned, then remove from the pan and set aside. Add the remaining oil and the spice paste, fry for 2–3 minutes, then add the cinnamon, cloves, star anise, cardamom and lemongrass and cook for another 2 minutes.

Return the browned beef to the pan, along with the toasted desiccated coconut, stir well, then add the coconut milk, tamarind paste, fish and soy sauces, lime leaves and beef stock and bring to the boil. Reduce the heat to a simmer, stirring regularly to make sure it doesn't stick. Cover with a lid and cook gently for 2 hours, until the meat is tender.

To make the coconut rice, place the rice, coconut milk and 400ml water into a heavy-based pan over a medium heat and bring to the boil. Reduce the heat to a simmer, then cover and cook for 10–12 minutes. Remove from the heat and allow to stand for a couple of minutes before serving.

Meanwhile, remove the lid from the beef and cook for another 15 minutes, until just thickened, then finish by adding the lime juice. Season with salt and pepper and serve with the coconut rice.

If there was ever the ultimate chefs' dish, this has to be it. Give me a bowl of beef ribs, a pile of chips and two hours of Coronation Street, and I'm a happy man! There's something almost primeval about gnawing the meat off the bones, and using beef ribs instead of pork means you get so much more to eat. They may look large when raw, but after simmering they reduce a lot in size.

Serves 4–6

1 onion

1 carrot

1.5kg beef fore ribs, cut into separate ribs

6 black peppercorns

3 bay leaves

1 small bunch fresh flat-leaf parsley

STICKY CHILLI SAUCE:

1 red chilli

200ml tomato ketchup

150ml chilli sauce

110ml dark soy sauce

175g honey

6 tbsp teriyaki sauce

5 tbsp bourbon whiskey

STICKY CHILLI-BRAISED BEEF RIBS

Roughly chop the onion and carrot. Place the beef ribs, peppercorns, bay leaves, parsley, onion and carrot into a large pan, cover with water and bring to the boil. When it comes to the boil, reduce the heat to a gentle simmer and cook very gently for 1½ hours, until very tender. Remove from the heat and allow to cool slightly.

Preheat the oven to 200°C/400°F/Gas mark 6. Finely chop the chilli. Place the tomato ketchup, chilli, soy sauce, chilli sauce, honey, teriyaki sauce and bourbon in a pan, stir well and bring to a simmer. Simmer for 3–4 minutes, then remove from the heat.

When the ribs have cooled, remove them from the liquid and dip them into the sticky chilli sauce or brush them generously with it, then place them in a roasting tin, reserving the remaining sauce. Roast for 10–12 minutes, then remove from the oven and spoon over more of the chilli sauce. Continue to roast for a further 10–12 minutes, then remove from the oven and serve with freshly cooked chips.

MADRAS CURRY POWDER:

1 cinnamon stick

3 dried red chillies

2 tbsp coriander seeds

1 tsp fenugreek seeds

1 tsp mustard seeds

1 tsp cumin seeds

2 tsp black peppercorns

5 curry leaves

2 tsp turmeric

LAMB MADRAS:

100g ghee or clarified butter
  (see method)

2 green bird's eye chillies

2 garlic cloves

a 2cm piece of fresh ginger

1kg lamb mince

3 onions

6 tomatoes

12 curry leaves

1 tsp salt

4 tbsp fresh coriander leaves

juice of ½ lemon

sea salt and freshly ground
  black pepper

Keema curries are made with minced meat. You can make this with the same quantity of diced lamb shoulder if you like, but mince is nice for a change. I worked with many Indian chefs during my time as a cook on cruise ships, and learnt many great recipes. This one was for 'staff chow', as they called it. It went on the stove when the restaurant started to slow down for the night, and we all dived in once we'd finished our shifts. Making your own curry powder is easy, and it's important here as the bought ones can vary a lot in quality.

KEEMA MADRAS CURRY

First, make the madras curry powder. Break the cinnamon stick into pieces. Heat a frying pan until medium hot, add all the spices and toast for 20–30 seconds, until just coloured. Tip them straight out into a spice grinder or pestle and mortar. Grind to a fine powder, then set aside.

If you need to make clarified butter, melt 150g butter in a small pan, then set aside to allow the solids to fall to the bottom of the pan. Skim the melted butter off the top and use it, discarding the solids.

To make the curry, finely chop the chillies, garlic and ginger. Place half the ghee or clarified butter, the chillies, garlic and ginger in a small food processor and process to a purée. Transfer to a bowl with the lamb mince and mix well to combine, then place in the fridge to marinate for at least 30 minutes.

Meanwhile, roughly chop the onions and tomatoes. Heat a large frying pan until hot, add the remaining ghee or clarified butter and the onions and cook over a medium heat for 20 minutes, until softened and brown, stirring occasionally. Increase the heat, add the lamb mince and cook until browned, stirring frequently, then add 3 tablespoons of the madras curry powder and the curry leaves and cook for another 2 minutes. Add the tomatoes, 150ml water and salt, and bring to the boil. Reduce the heat to a simmer and cook over a low heat for 1½ hours, until tender and just thickened.

Chop the coriander leaves, then add them to the curry with the lemon juice. Season with salt and pepper if needed, then serve with some plain steamed rice, poppadoms and mango chutney.

Serves 4

1 large onion

3 garlic cloves

1 tbsp olive oil

1.5kg diced skinless leg of pork

1 tsp caraway seeds

2 tsp sweet smoked paprika

½ tsp cayenne pepper

1 tbsp tomato purée

2 x 400g tins chopped tomatoes

300ml beef stock

300g long-grain rice

2 tsp chopped fresh chives

sea salt and freshly ground
  black pepper

Although it is traditionally cooked with beef, goulash is also a great dish with pork. It seemed to be on everyone's menus in the 1980s (along with chicken Kiev and crêpes Suzette), but it tastes great, even though it doesn't look it. I've done it with rice here, but in Hungary it's often eaten with potatoes or buttered noodles, and it's sometimes even served as a soup.

HUNGARIAN PORK GOULASH

Finely chop the onion and crush the garlic. Heat a heavy-based pan over a medium heat, add the olive oil and pork and fry until browned all over. Remove the meat from the pan and set aside, then drain off any excess fat. Add the onion, garlic and caraway seeds and sweat for 5–10 minutes, until softened.

Meanwhile, mix the paprika and cayenne together, then toss it with the browned pork pieces. Return the pork to the pan and stir well. Add the tomato purée and stir well, then cook for about 4–5 minutes. Add the tomatoes and stock, bring to the boil, then reduce the heat to a simmer, part-cover with a lid and cook for about 3 hours, stirring occasionally.

About 25 minutes before the end of the cooking time for the goulash, place the rice in a saucepan and cover with 300ml water. Bring to the boil, then reduce to a very gentle simmer, cover with a lid and cook for about 20 minutes.

When the rice is cooked, turn the heat off and season with salt and pepper. Spoon the rice into the serving bowls along with a large ladleful of goulash and a sprinkling of chopped chives.

You often see blanquette de veau in French bistros. It's usually served with rice or pasta, but it can be served with potatoes too. Unlike most stews, the meat isn't browned, as this will make the sauce darker. True veal blanquette should be white.

Serves 4–6

1 kg diced shoulder of veal

1 carrot

1 small onion

1 clove

1 large fresh thyme sprig

1 bay leaf

100g baby onions

50g butter

25g plain flour

4 slices white bread

a drizzle of rapeseed oil

1 large fresh flat-leaf parsley sprig

100g button mushrooms

4 egg yolks

100ml double cream

sea salt and freshly ground
  black pepper

VEAL BLANQUETTE

Put the veal in a large saucepan and cover with 2.2 litres water. Add the carrot, onion, clove, thyme and bay leaf and bring to a gentle simmer, then reduce the heat and cook gently for 1¼ hours. When the meat is tender, remove from the heat, drain and reserve it, along with 1 litre of the cooking liquid, then set aside. Discard the remaining liquid, along with the vegetables and herbs. Peel the whole baby onions (see page 133).

Heat a large, heavy-based pan over a medium heat, add half the butter and melt it, then add the flour and stir until it is completely absorbed. Gradually whisk in the reserved cooking liquid. Add the meat to the sauce and keep it warm over a very low heat. Season with salt and pepper.

Cut the bread into crustless triangles. Heat a frying pan until hot, add the rapeseed oil and fry the triangles on one side until golden brown. Add a little of the remaining butter, then turn the triangles over and cook until a nice, even golden-brown colour. Remove and drain on kitchen paper. Chop the parsley and sprinkle a little of it over the triangles. Quarter the mushrooms. Heat a frying pan over a medium heat, add the rest of the butter and the onions and cook until lightly coloured. Add the mushrooms and cook for 2 minutes, then add the mushrooms and onions to the veal.

Whisk the egg yolks and cream together in a small bowl, then gradually add to the pan with the veal, whisking as you go. Remove from the heat and continue whisking for 2 minutes. Just before serving, sprinkle the veal with the remaining parsley and place the triangles of fried bread on top.

slow
puddings

This is good, proper comfort food, and was a massive hit after the photograph was taken. Quick fruit jams are full of flavour, and cooking them quickly means you keep more of the freshness. Unlike school-dinner rice pudding, this one is light and tasty and won't hold up textbooks or stop the school bus rolling down the hill. Eating the skin on the top is the chef's perk!

Serves 4

RICE PUDDING:

50g butter

125g pudding rice or paella rice

75g caster sugar

½ vanilla pod

750ml full-fat milk

150ml double cream

a pinch of salt

a pinch of freshly grated nutmeg

STRAWBERRY JAM:

250g strawberries

250g caster sugar

juice of ½ lemon

BAKED RICE PUDDING WITH QUICK STRAWBERRY JAM

Preheat the oven to 150°C/300°F/Gas mark 2. Melt the butter in a heavy-based casserole dish over a medium heat, add the rice and stir to coat it. Add the sugar and keep stirring until it becomes sticky. Split the vanilla pod in half lengthways and scrape out the seeds. Pour the milk and cream into the rice and keep stirring, adding the vanilla pod and seeds, salt and nutmeg. Taste the mixture to make sure it's as sweet as you'd like it to be.

Stop stirring, then grate a little more nutmeg over the top and bake in the oven for 1 hour. If it colours too quickly, cover the dish with foil. If the pudding just wobbles slightly in the centre, it is ready. Remove from the oven and allow to cool a little while you make the quick strawberry jam.

Cut the stalks off the strawberries and cut any large ones in half. Heat the sugar, strawberries and lemon juice in a large saucepan over a medium heat until the sugar has melted. Bring the mixture to the boil and cook for 3–4 minutes (or up to 10 minutes if you prefer a thicker jam). Check the temperature with a sugar thermometer – it should reach 105°C (220°F).

Allow the jam to cool slightly and skim off any froth from the top with a clean spoon. If you want to keep the jam, spoon it into sterilized jam jars (see page 35), seal and label them, and it will keep for 2–3 months. Serve the jam in a pot with the warm rice pudding.

Who doesn't like strawberries, meringue and cream? And it's even better when they're all combined together. This dish can be made with fresh strawberries or raspberries – either way, during cooking they leak out a gooey mixture that adds to the flavour even more.

Serves 4

550g strawberries

4 egg whites

110g caster sugar

110g icing sugar, sifted, plus 20g
  for the sauce

250ml double cream

STRAWBERRY MERINGUES
WITH CREAM

Preheat the oven to 100°C/200°F/Gas mark ¼ and line a baking sheet with baking parchment. Hull the strawberries and cut them in half. Beat the egg whites with the caster sugar in a grease-free bowl until stiff peaks form. Add the 110g icing sugar and continue to beat for 4–6 minutes, or until the mixture is smooth and shiny.

Using a large metal spoon, fold just under half of the strawberries lightly into the meringue mixture. With the same spoon, carefully place 8 even-sized spoonfuls of the mixture onto the sheet. Bake in the oven for 2 hours.

While the meringues are cooking, place the remaining strawberries, 3 tablespoons water and the 20g icing sugar in a blender and process to a purée, then pass it through a sieve to remove the seeds. Set aside.

When the meringues are cooked, remove them from the oven and allow to cool slightly before removing from the baking sheet using a palette knife. Transfer to a wire cooling rack and set aside. Place the double cream in a bowl and whip until soft peaks form, then serve along with the meringues and the strawberry sauce.

A slow food cookbook woudn't be complete without this recipe in it. Rather than reinvent the wheel, it's just a great, plain old steamed sponge pudding with a bit of stem ginger. Don't forget the custard!

Serves 6

50g stem ginger

175g soft butter, plus extra
   for greasing

4 tbsp golden syrup, warmed

175g soft light brown sugar

3 eggs

175g self-raising flour

1 tsp ground ginger

1 rounded tsp baking powder

STEAMED GINGER
SPONGE PUDDING

Finely chop the stem ginger. Grease a 1.2-litre heatproof pudding basin with butter and pour the golden syrup into the bottom. Put the sugar and butter in a mixing bowl and beat with a hand-held electric whisk until light and fluffy. Add the eggs one at a time, then add the stem ginger and beat well. Fold in the flour, ground ginger and baking powder. Pour the pudding mixture into the basin and level the top.

Cut out a circle of greaseproof paper the same diameter as the pudding basin and place it on top of the pudding. Put the basin onto a clean tea towel or muslin cloth and lift it up around the sides. Tie the tops together with a piece of string, then place the basin into a large pan and fill it half full with water.

Cover with a lid, bring to the boil, then reduce the heat and steam gently for 2 hours, checking the water level halfway through. Once cooked, turn the heat off and allow to cool slightly before taking out of the pan. Remove the cloth and greaseproof paper. Put a plate on top, then turn the basin over and leave it for 1–2 minutes before lifting the basin off to reveal the pudding. Serve with fresh custard.

This combination of flavours works really well in all manner of desserts, and not just cheesecakes. This is one of my favourites in the whole book. If you can avoid it, don't chill the cheesecake in the fridge, as it sometimes goes grainy.

Serves 6

150g walnut, hazelnut or
  macadamia cookies

50g butter

1 vanilla pod

200g caster sugar

4 tbsp cornflour

850g full-fat soft cream cheese

4 eggs

150ml cold strong coffee

375ml double cream

100g chocolate buttons

COFFEE, WALNUT AND CHOCOLATE CHEESECAKE

Preheat the oven to 170°C/325°F/Gas mark 3. Put the cookies in a food processor and process to fine crumbs. Melt the butter in a small pan, then add to the crumbs and process once more. Press the crumb mixture into the base and sides of a 23cm springform cake tin.

Split the vanilla pod in half lengthways, scrape out the seeds and put them in a bowl with the sugar, cornflour and cream cheese, and whisk together. Add the eggs, one at a time, beating well between each one, then add the coffee. Add the double cream, whisking until the mixture is smooth, then fold in the chocolate buttons. Pour the mixture into the cake tin and tap lightly to settle the mix.

Place the cake tin in a roasting tin, then pour hot water into the tin to a depth of 2cm to create a bain marie. Bake in the oven for 1–1¼ hours, until the top is golden and the cheesecake is just set – there will be a slight wobble in the centre. Remove from the oven and allow to cool in the tin before cutting and serving with a drizzle of double cream.

Lemon tart is a real chef's pudding. This orange version makes a nice change, and it's great to use oranges when they're in season. The trick is to make sure the pastry is nice and thin and cooked through, and not to let the filling leak. I love serving it in the restaurant, but I equally enjoy teaching and watching people cook it.

Serves 6–8

4 unwaxed oranges

6 eggs

200g caster sugar

325ml double cream

plain flour, for dusting

icing sugar, for dusting (optional)

500g sweet shortcrust pastry
  (see page 178)

ORANGE TART

Finely grate the zest and squeeze the juice of the oranges – you need about 300ml orange juice. Reserve the zest. Whisk the eggs and sugar in a large bowl until combined. Add the double cream and orange juice and whisk again. Cover and place in the fridge overnight to infuse. The next day, pour the mixture through a sieve into a jug, and then stir in the orange zest.

Roll the pastry out on a lightly floured work surface to a circle 5mm thick and about 30cm in diameter. Roll the pastry over the rolling pin, then transfer to a 22cm diameter, 6cm deep tart tin. Line the tin with the pastry, pressing it carefully into the edges, making sure the pastry hangs at least 2cm over the rim. Put in the fridge to chill for 30 minutes. Preheat the oven to 180°C/350°F/Gas mark 4.

Line the pastry case with greaseproof paper and fill it with baking beans, rice or flour. Put the tin onto a baking sheet and bake for 15 minutes. Remove the paper and contents and bake the empty pastry case for a further 10 minutes. Carefully trim off the overhanging pastry edge so it is level with the top of the tin.

Reduce the oven temperature to 100°C/200°F/Gas mark ¼. Pour the filling mixture into the pastry case. Transfer to the oven and bake the tart for 1½ hours, or until the filling is just set. Remove the tart from the oven and allow to cool for about 1 hour before removing from the tin. Glaze with a kitchen blowtorch until lightly browned, or dust with a little icing sugar. Serve with crème fraîche.

'Ensaimadas', or traditional coiled pastries, are popular all over the Balearics, and this recipe is a twist on one I discovered in Ibiza. It was called 'ensaimadas con cabello de angel', and was filled with a pumpkin jam made by mixing cooked pumpkin with sugar, which changes the texture of the jam to a stringy mixture, hence the reference to angel's hair. It is made using lard or olive oil, but lard is the best thing to use in terms of flavour, although I know it seems strange! You can use butter if you prefer.

Serves 4–6

500g butternut squash

350g caster sugar

juice of ½ lemon

250g filo pastry

a pinch of freshly grated nutmeg

100g melted lard

icing sugar, for dusting

BUTTERNUT FILO WHIRL

Peel and cut the butternut squash into rough dice. Heat a saucepan until medium hot, add 300g of the caster sugar and 50ml water and cook until the sugar has melted. Add the squash and stir well, then cover and simmer for 10 minutes. Remove the lid and simmer for a further 15 minutes, until the liquid has thickened and the squash has softened. Remove from the heat and add the lemon juice and nutmeg. Beat well until smooth, then allow to cool.

Preheat the oven to 170°C/325°F/Gas mark 3. Line a large baking tray with baking parchment. Place the filo pastry on a clean work surface and cut it into a 50 x 30cm rectangle, and brush it with the melted lard. Spoon the squash mixture in a line about 7.5cm below the long top edge, covering the top third of the pastry. Carefully fold the top long edge over the squash to cover it. Sprinkle the remaining caster sugar over the rest of the pastry. Roll the pastry towards you to make a loose Swiss roll shape. Transfer to the baking tray and curve it around to form a horseshoe shape.

Bake in the oven for 1 hour, until golden, crispy and cooked through. Remove from the oven and allow to cool slightly before dusting with icing sugar. Cut into thick slices to serve.

Who can resist this? I recently served it at a dinner party some 20 years after the last time I made it, and it was a big hit. With recipes, you sometimes have to look back to go forward. My gran used to call it dead man's arm because she used to use one of my granddad's old shirt sleeves to cook it in – although he was still alive!

Serves 4–6

500g self-raising flour, plus extra
  for dusting

100g caster sugar

250g shredded suet

grated zest of 2 unwaxed lemons

200g raspberry jam

JAM ROLY POLY

Place the flour, sugar, suet and lemon zest in a bowl and mix thoroughly. Make a well in the centre, then gradually add about 250ml water, enough to form a soft dough. Knead lightly until smooth.

Turn onto a lightly floured surface and roll out to an oblong shape about 1cm thick. Spread the jam out over the dough, leaving a 2.5cm gap around the edges. Roll it up from the long side to form a Swiss roll shape. Put it on a large sheet of foil and roll the foil around it carefully, leaving some room for expansion, then twist the ends to seal. Place in an old shirt sleeve or wrap in a clean cloth and tie the ends. Put some kitchen paper or a cloth in the base of a large pan, then put an upturned loaf tin or rectangular plate on top of it. Put the roly poly on top, then add enough hot water so that the roly poly sits just clear of the water.

Cover with a lid or foil, place over a medium-low heat and steam for 1½ hours, topping up the water as necessary. Turn off the heat and leave the pudding to stand for 5 minutes before carefully removing the sleeve and foil. Carve into slices and serve with custard or ice cream.

Serves 6–8

PASTRY:

175g butter, plus extra for greasing

240g plain flour, plus extra
  for dusting

50g icing sugar

1 egg yolk

FILLING:

1 vanilla pod

750ml double cream

10 egg yolks

2 whole eggs

100g caster sugar

¼ tsp freshly grated nutmeg

I remember that when I was young, aged around seven or eight, I used to save my dinner and tuck shop money and head to Thomas the Bakers on my way home. They had small custard tarts that I used to love – it was probably right there and then that my sweet tooth began. Fresh vanilla pods and nutmeg are the key to this for me.

BAKED EGG CUSTARD TART

Grease and flour a 23cm diameter, 4cm deep tart tin. Sift the flour and icing sugar in a mixing bowl and stir together. Cut the butter into cubes and rub it together with your fingertips until it resembles breadcrumbs. Add the egg yolk and about 4 tablespoons water, a little at a time, and keep mixing to form a soft dough. Remove it from the bowl and flatten it into a disc. Wrap it in clingfilm and chill in the fridge for at least 30 minutes.

For the filling, split the vanilla pod in half lengthways and scrape the seeds out into a bowl. Add the rest of the filling ingredients, reserving one of the egg yolks for later, and whisk together, then pass through a fine sieve and set aside.

Remove the pastry from the fridge and roll it out on a lightly floured work surface to make a disc roughly 40cm in diameter. Place the pastry into the tart tin, pressing down lightly so that the tin is lined with no gaps, and leave a little pastry hanging over the rim. Return to the fridge to rest for about 15 minutes. Preheat the oven to 180°C/350°F/Gas mark 4.

Line the pastry case with greaseproof paper and baking beans, rice or flour and bake in the oven for 15 minutes. Remove the paper and contents, then brush the base and sides of the pastry case with the reserved beaten egg yolk, making sure there are no holes anywhere. Return the tart case to the oven and bake for another 10 minutes, until just coloured.

Reduce the temperature to 100°C/200°F/Gas mark ¼, then slide out the oven shelf the pastry case is on. Carefully pour the custard mixture into the pastry case and gently slide it back into the oven. Bake for 1 hour, then turn the oven off and let the tart completely cool in the oven before serving.

Serves 8–10

PASTRY:

200g plain flour, plus extra
   for dusting

½ tsp sea salt

2 tbsp icing sugar

100g butter, plus extra for greasing

1 egg

1 tsp lemon juice

FILLING:

90g walnuts

90g ground almonds

50g plain flour

225g butter, softened

225g caster sugar

4 eggs

4–5 large pears

Pear and almond is a combination we're used to, but the other day some wet (or just-picked) walnuts arrived in the restaurant, and I couldn't resist making this. French walnut liqueur would be delicious in this dessert if you come across it. Serve it with double cream, or, if it's still warm, a scoop of ice cream.

PEAR AND WALNUT TART

First make the pastry. Mix the flour, salt and icing sugar into a bowl. Add half the butter and rub into the flour with your fingertips until it resembles coarse breadcrumbs. Add the rest of the butter and rub it in until it looks like small peas. Mix the egg, lemon juice and 2 tablespoons iced water together and add it to the flour mixture gradually until it forms a dough. Turn out onto a floured work surface and knead lightly until smooth, shape into a flat disc, cover in clingfilm and chill in the fridge for 30 minutes.

Lightly grease and flour a 26cm diameter, 4cm deep, fluted, loose-bottomed tart tin. Remove the pastry from the fridge and roll it out on a lightly floured surface to a 5mm thick circle, about 40cm in diameter. Using the rolling pin, transfer it to the tin. Press down lightly all over the base and sides of the tin, easing any overlapping pastry back down the sides. Trim the pastry, leaving at least 2cm above the rim. Put in the fridge for 30 minutes.

Preheat the oven to 180°C/350°F/Gas mark 4. Line the pastry case with greaseproof paper and fill with baking beans, rice or flour. Put on a baking sheet and bake for 15 minutes, then remove the paper and contents. Return to the oven for 10 minutes.

Reduce the temperature to 150°C/300°F/Gas mark 2. Put the walnuts in a food processor and process until very fine, then add the ground almonds and flour and pulse to combine. Set aside. Cream the butter and sugar in a mixing bowl until very pale and fluffy. Beat 1 egg at a time into the butter mixture, adding a handful of the nut mixture after each addition, until all the eggs have been added. Add the remaining nut mixture and fold together.

Peel the pears, halve and remove the cores, then cut into quarters. Place the pear quarters in the tart case in a circle shape to fill the base. Spoon the mixture over the top and smooth it over. Place on a baking tray in the oven and cook for 1 hour, until golden and risen. When cooked, remove from the oven and leave to cool in the tin for 15 minutes. Remove the tart from the tin and cut it into wedges, then serve with a dollop of cream.

New Yorkers get this right, and their cheesecake should only be changed in terms of the flavouring. Don't tamper with something that works! It's best to serve this at room temperature, as I find that straight from the fridge it's a bit like listening to your bank manager – hard work and not very pleasant!

Serves 6–8

1 x 23cm sponge base

1 vanilla pod

grated zest and juice of
  1 unwaxed lemon

200g caster sugar

50g cornflour

850g full-fat soft cream cheese

4 large eggs

375ml double cream

400g raspberries

150ml maple syrup

BAKED NEW YORK RASPBERRY CHEESECAKE

Preheat the oven to 180°C/350°F/Gas mark 4. Cut the sponge base to a diameter of 23cm if necessary, then slice in half horizontally to form a 5mm thick disc, and place it in the bottom of a springform 23cm cake tin.

Split the vanilla pod in half lengthways and scrape out the seeds. Put the vanilla seeds, lemon zest and juice, sugar, cornflour and cream cheese into a bowl and whisk together. Add the eggs, one at a time, beating well between each one. Add the double cream, whisking until the mixture is smooth, then add 250g of the raspberries and stir carefully through the mixture.

Pour the mixture into the cake tin and tap it lightly to settle the mix. Put the cake tin into a roasting tray, then pour hot water into the tray to a depth of 2cm to create a bain marie. Bake for 1¼– 1½ hours, until the top is golden and the cheesecake is just set.

Remove from the oven and allow to cool in the tin. Remove and place on a serving plate, then top with the remaining raspberries and drizzle over the maple syrup. Serve with a drizzle of double cream.

This recipe goes to show that everyone can learn new dishes, even French chefs, as I discovered when I met some people who had opened a restaurant in Paris serving exactly this. Some people cook the filling beforehand and add the crumble over the top, and others do it this way. I think that if you have the time in the oven, this is the better of the two. The secret is to cut the apples into large pieces, and as it cooks the crumble and the filling will go crisp around the edges.

Serves 6–8

4 Bramley apples

200g demerara sugar

300g blackberries

175g plain flour

50g ground almonds

1 tsp ground mixed spice

150g butter

50g flaked almonds

APPLE AND BLACKBERRY CRUMBLE

Preheat the oven to 150°C/300°F/Gas mark 2. Peel and core the apples, cut them into quarters and put them in a 22 x 28cm deep-sided baking dish. Dust with a little of the sugar, then place the blackberries on top and set aside.

Put the rest of the sugar, flour, ground almonds and mixed spice into a bowl and stir together. Cut the butter into cubes and rub it into the flour with your fingertips until it resembles breadcrumbs. Scatter the mixture over the top of the fruit, sprinkle over the flaked almonds, and cook in the oven for 1 hour, until golden and bubbling. Remove and allow to cool for 5 minutes before serving with pouring cream.

This has got to be one of my favourite puddings in the book. For me, it's the best dinner party dish because not only does it look great, but once made it can be stored in the fridge for a few hours, where the meringue will go all sticky and delicious. It freezes well, too. If you like, you could top it with some caramelized nuts or fresh strawberries.

Serves 6–8

8 egg whites

375g white caster sugar

grated zest and juice of
  4 unwaxed lemons

100g butter

4 whole eggs, lightly beaten

400ml double cream

8 passion fruit

2–3 tbsp icing sugar

MERINGUE, LEMON CURD AND PASSION FRUIT TORTE

Preheat the oven to 100°C/200°F/Gas mark ¼. Draw 3 x 25cm diameter circles on sheets of baking parchment and place them on baking sheets. Put the egg whites in a grease-free bowl and whisk until soft peaks form. Gradually add 200g caster sugar and continue to whisk until stiff peaks form. Put a little blob of meringue under the edges of the baking parchment to secure it. Spoon some meringue onto each circle and spread it out to make a disc, flattening lightly with the back of the spoon. Cook in the oven for 20 minutes. Turn the oven off, leaving the meringues inside for 2 hours, or preferably overnight. When crisp, remove from the oven.

Make the lemon curd. Put the lemon zest and juice in a heatproof bowl, then add the butter and remaining caster sugar, stir well, and set over a pan of simmering water. Whisk until totally dissolved, then beat in the whole eggs and whisk until thickened and cooked through. Remove from the heat and cool over a bowl of ice, whisking occasionally until completely cold.

Whip the double cream in a large bowl until soft peaks form, then gently fold in the lemon curd. Scoop out the seeds of 6 of the passion fruit and fold lightly into the cream.

To assemble, place a meringue disc on a serving plate, then top with half the lemon curd cream. Place a second disc on top and spread over the rest of the cream. Place the last disc on top and press very lightly to settle, then scoop out the seeds from the remaining passion fruit and spoon over the top. Dust with a little icing sugar and cut into wedges to serve.

I learnt this dish while working in a brasserie in the south of France, where I was training. This kind of pudding never seems to be on the menu in restaurants any more, but I don't know why: I always order it whenever I see it on the menu. This recipe is 28 years old, but the dish is much older than that, and it's a true classic.

Serves 6

325g caster sugar

1 vanilla pod

50g stem ginger

800ml milk

200ml double cream

4 whole eggs

6 egg yolks

250g strawberries

BAKED CRÈME CARAMEL WITH STRAWBERRIES

Place 200g of the sugar and 75ml water in a clean, non-stick pan over a gentle heat to melt. Do not stir. When it's an even golden-brown colour, remove from the heat and carefully add 75ml water, standing well back. Allow to cool slightly, then carefully pour the caramel into a 2-litre ovenproof glass bowl.

Preheat the oven to 140°C/275°F/Gas mark 1. Split the vanilla pod in half lengthways and scrape out the seeds. Finely grate the stem ginger. Put the milk, cream, ginger, vanilla pod and seeds in a pan and heat to simmering point over a low heat.

Put the remaining sugar, eggs and egg yolks in a large bowl and whisk until just combined. Pour the hot milk and cream mixture onto the eggs and whisk together. Spoon off any foam that has formed and strain the mixture into the caramel-lined bowl. Place it in a deep, ovenproof roasting tin and fill with enough water to come 5cm up the side of the bowl. Bake in the oven for 1¾ hours.

Remove from the oven and allow to cool. Transfer to the fridge for at least 2 hours to cool completely. Heat a shallow pan of water to a gentle simmer and put the crème caramel in it until the caramel softens, then turn upside down onto a serving plate. Remove the stalks from the strawberries and serve them piled on top of the crème caramel.

This is a simple idea, but I love it. It can be served hot, straight from the oven, or cooled, and it's gooey in the centre when you spoon it out. I love it because it's crusted on top and set like a mousse underneath, so you get the best of both textures. You can use the same filling in a tart, but in a pot like this it's so much easier and quicker. Serve on its own, or with cream and cherries.

Serves 4

250g milk chocolate

100g dark chocolate

600ml double cream

4 large eggs

3 tbsp Amaretto liqueur

50g caster sugar

2 tsp vanilla sugar

BAKED CHOCOLATE POT

Preheat the oven to 150°C/300°F/Gas mark 2. Break the milk and dark chocolate into pieces and place in a heavy-based saucepan with 400ml of the cream. Cook over a gentle heat, stirring constantly, until the chocolate melts. Remove from the heat, continuing to stir.

Put the eggs, Amaretto liqueur and sugar in a separate bowl and mix well, but do not whisk. Pour the warm chocolate mixture onto the eggs, then stir until incorporated and pour through a fine sieve into a measuring jug.

Put a tea towel in a deep roasting tin along with 4 individual ovenproof serving cups or ramekins, about 7.5cm tall and 4cm deep. Pour the chocolate mixture into them and put the tray in the oven on the middle shelf. Pour hot tap water into the tray until it comes up halfway up the sides of the serving cups, then close the oven door and bake for 1 hour.

Remove from the oven and serve warm, or allow to cool before taking out of the tray. Put in the fridge to cool for 1 hour. Place the remaining cream in a mixing bowl with the vanilla sugar. Whip until soft peaks form, then serve alongside the chocolate pots.

A bowl of custard with a few sliced bananas has to be one of the great comfort dishes. More of a pudding than a tart, this recipe includes all the same flavours. The trick is to cook the custard mixture carefully, as overcooking any egg custard can cause it to split and separate.

Serves 8

PASTRY:

225g plain flour, plus extra
   for dusting

50g caster sugar

125g butter, slightly softened

1 egg, plus 1 egg yolk

1 vanilla pod

FILLING:

5–6 bananas

2 eggs, plus 4 egg yolks

100g caster sugar

1 vanilla pod

800ml double cream

BANANA AND CUSTARD TART

First make the pastry. Rub the flour, sugar and butter together until they resemble breadcrumbs. Lightly beat the whole egg, split the vanilla pod in half lengthways and scrape out the seeds. Stir the egg and vanilla seeds into the flour and butter mixture, then knead it gently to form a dough. Shape into a disc, then cover with clingfilm and chill in the fridge for 30 minutes.

Roll the pastry out on a lightly floured work surface into a 3mm thick circle, about 30cm in diameter. Use the rolling pin to transfer it to a 24cm diameter, 6cm deep tart tin. Line the tin with the pastry, pressing carefully into the edges, making sure it hangs at least 2cm over the rim. Chill in the fridge for 30 minutes. Preheat the oven to 180°C/350°F/Gas mark 4.

Line the pastry case with greaseproof paper and fill it with baking beans, rice or flour. Put the tin on a baking tray and bake for 15 minutes. Remove the paper and contents and bake for a further 5 minutes. Beat the egg yolk. Carefully trim off the overhanging pastry edge level with the top of the tin, then brush the inside of the case with the egg yolk to seal the pastry. Put it back in the oven for a further 5 minutes, then remove from the oven.

Reduce the temperature to 150°C/300°F/Gas mark 2. Peel the bananas and put them in the base of the tart case to fill the bottom. In a bowl, beat together the eggs, egg yolks and sugar. Split the vanilla pod in half lengthways and scrape out the seeds. Bring the cream and vanilla seeds to the boil in a small pan. Once boiling, whisk the cream into the egg mixture, beating all the time. Pour this into the pastry case over the bananas and bake for 1½ hours, until the mixture has set and is just golden brown.

Not so dainty to eat, this pudding has a little surprise in the bottom: a pool of sugary lemon mixture. Its origins aren't clear – some say it's American, some say French, while others believe its source is British. Wherever it's from, there's no denying that it's a simple, great-tasting dessert.

Serves 6

25g soft butter, plus extra
  for greasing

150g caster sugar

50g plain flour

2 eggs, separated

200ml milk

grated zest and juice of
  1 unwaxed lemon

DAINTY PUDDING

Preheat the oven to 150°C/300°F/Gas mark 2. Grease a 1-litre flat pie dish, making sure the corners are well buttered, and put it in the fridge.

Put the butter and sugar into a bowl and whisk until pale and fluffy. Fold in the flour, then add the egg yolks, lemon zest and juice and milk, and whisk until combined. Whisk the egg whites in a separate bowl until soft peaks form, then fold into the mixture one third at a time.

Pour the mixture into the pie dish, then put it in a deep-sided roasting tin and pour hot water into the tin until it comes halfway up the sides of the pie dish. Bake in the oven for 1 hour, until it springs back slightly when you press lightly on top. Remove from the oven and allow to cool slightly before serving. Serve with cream.

Serves 8

PASTRY:

225g plain flour, plus extra
for dusting

50g caster sugar

125g soft butter, plus extra
for greasing

1 vanilla pod

1 egg, plus 1 egg yolk

FILLING:

1 red chilli

50g pecan halves

50g almond halves

50g shelled pistachios

50g cashew nuts

50g macadamia nuts

50g hazelnuts

50g brazil nuts

½ tsp celery salt

1½ tsp tandoori powder

150g caster sugar

1 tbsp Worcestershire sauce

200g dark chocolate,
70% cocoa solids

350ml double cream

2 eggs

1 tsp flaky sea salt

When I first heard about this dish I had nightmare visions of putting salted peanuts in a dessert! But then I got the idea and realized that the mixture of sweetened chilli nuts with chocolate would be great. The secret is not to overcook the chocolate mixture.

SPICED CHOCOLATE AND NUT TART

Rub the flour, sugar and butter together until they resemble breadcrumbs. Split the vanilla pod in half lengthways and scrape out the seeds. Stir the egg and vanilla seeds into the mixture with a spoon, then knead gently to form a dough. Press into a disc shape, cover with clingfilm and put in the fridge for 30 minutes. Grease and flour a 24 x 4cm tart tin. Roll the pastry out on a lightly floured surface to a 3mm thick circle, about 30cm diameter. Use the rolling pin to transfer it to the tin. Line the tin with the pastry, pressing it carefully into the edges, making sure it hangs at least 2cm over the rim. Put into the fridge to chill for 30 minutes.

Preheat the oven to 180°C/350°F/Gas mark 4. Line the pastry case with greaseproof paper and fill it with baking beans, rice or flour. Put the tin on a baking sheet and bake for 15 minutes. Remove the paper and contents and bake the pastry case for a further 5 minutes. Carefully trim off the overhanging pastry so it is level with the top of the tin, then brush the inside with the beaten egg yolk to seal the pastry. Return to the oven for a further 5 minutes to seal it, then remove from the oven.

Finely chop the chilli. Heat a frying pan until hot, add the nuts and toss to combine. Add the chilli, celery salt and tandoori powder and mix well, then cook for 30 seconds. Add half the sugar and cook until it starts to caramelize, then add the Worcestershire sauce and carefully toss once more so that all the nuts are coated in the spiced sugar mixture. Pour onto a baking sheet and leave to cool, then break up into individual pieces.

Break the chocolate into pieces and put it in a heatproof bowl over a pan of barely simmering water. Heat gently until melted. Remove from the heat, then whisk in the double cream, eggs and remaining sugar and set aside.

Reduce the oven temperature to 120°C/250°F/Gas mark ½. Tip the nuts into the tart case and spread them out. Pour the chocolate over the top. Tap the tray gently so it levels the mixture, then bake in the oven for 1 hour. When cooked, remove from the oven and sprinkle the salt over the top. Allow to cool completely before removing from the tin. Cut into wedges and serve with a dollop of sour cream.

slow
bakes

You'll need to start this one the day before, I'm afraid, but it's simple. The use of tea in a fruit loaf isn't new, but it makes a great cake. This recipe has been in my family for years, which is why we use Yorkshire tea.

Serves 8

160g sultanas

160g currants

160g raisins

50g diced mixed candied peel

160g demerara sugar

175ml strong Yorkshire or
  Earl Grey tea

butter, for greasing

65g walnuts

2 eggs

75ml double cream

300g self-raising flour

FRUITED IRISH TEA LOAF

Put all the dried fruit into a bowl, add the sugar and pour over the hot tea, stir well then cover and leave overnight to infuse.

Preheat the oven to 170°C/325°F/Gas mark 3 and lightly grease a 1kg loaf tin, then line it with baking parchment. The butter will help you to do this by making it stick. Roughly chop the walnuts, add them to the fruit and stir well.

Whisk together the eggs and double cream, then stir in the fruit. Sift the flour into the mixture and stir well with a large wooden spoon until it is well combined. Spoon the mixture into the prepared tin and spread the top as flat as you can. Bake in the middle of the oven for 70–80 minutes, until the top springs back when lightly pressed. Check if the cake is cooked by inserting a clean skewer or knife into the centre – if it comes out clean, the cake is ready. If not, bake for a further 10 minutes and check once more.

Remove from the oven and allow to cool before removing from the tin and leaving to cool completely on a wire cooling rack. Serve in slices, buttered, on its own or with some jam, such as strawberry.

I first made this when I was in Valencia, southern Spain, which of course is famous for oranges and saffron. Boiling the oranges makes the mixture a bit different – it produces a moist texture rather like a polenta cake. Saffron should always be used sparingly, particularly in desserts, as the flavour is very strong.

Serves 8–10

butter, for greasing

650g whole unwaxed oranges

400g caster sugar

300g ground almonds

6 eggs

1 tbsp baking powder

1 heaped tsp Chinese five-spice powder

2 good pinches of saffron threads

50g blanched whole almonds

juice of 1 orange

BOILED ORANGE AND SAFFRON CAKE

Preheat the oven to 170°C/325°F/Gas mark 3. Lightly grease a 23cm diameter springform cake tin. Wash the oranges thoroughly, then put them in a large saucepan and cover with cold water. Bring to the boil over a medium heat, reduce to a simmer, cover and cook for 25 minutes. Remove from the heat and allow to cool.

Remove the cooled oranges and cut them in half, discarding any pips. Roughly chop them, then put them in a food processor along with 250g of the sugar, the ground almonds, eggs, baking powder, five-spice powder and saffron and process to a purée, scraping down the sides of the bowl.

Pour the mixture into the prepared tin and bake in the oven for 1½ hours. Check if the cake is cooked by inserting a clean skewer or knife into the centre – if it comes out clean, the cake is ready. If not, bake for a further 10 minutes and check once more.

Meanwhile, for the decoration, put the remaining sugar in a saucepan along with 1 tablespoon water and gently heat through. Cook until the sugar is syrupy, then add the whole almonds and cook for a couple of minutes more. Remove the almonds with a slotted spoon and place on a wire cooling rack, then add the orange juice to the syrup and heat through.

When the cake is cooked, remove from the oven and allow to cool in the tin for 20 minutes before turning out. Pour the orange syrup over the cake, then scatter the almonds over the top.

This all-in-one method is simple: just place everything in a bowl, blitz it together and add the fruit. It's a bit like my gran's old lardy cake recipe, a great base to which many other types of fruit can be added.

Serves 6–8

125g soft butter, plus extra
  for greasing

250g plain flour, plus extra
  for dusting

1 tsp baking powder

1 tbsp mixed spice

150g soft brown sugar

2 large eggs

150g dessert apples

150g dried apricots

150g skinned pistachios

APPLE, APRICOT AND PISTACHIO LOAF

Preheat the oven to 150°C/300°F/Gas mark 2. Grease a 1kg loaf tin and dust it with flour, tapping out any excess. Put the flour, baking powder, spice, butter, sugar and eggs in a large bowl and whisk with an electric hand whisk on a low speed until well combined.

Peel, core and chop the apples into 1cm dice. Chop the dried apricots. Add the apples and apricots to the cake mixture along with the pistachios, and fold them in with a spoon until just combined.

Pour the mixture into the prepared loaf tin and bake in the oven. If using a long, shallow loaf tin, bake for 1 hour. If using a short, deep loaf tin, increase the cooking time to 1½ hours. Check if the cake is cooked by inserting a clean skewer or knife into the centre – if it comes out clean, the cake is ready. If not, bake for a further 5 minutes and check once more. Repeat until the skewer comes out clean.

Leave in the tin to cool for at least 30 minutes before turning out, then allow to cool to room temperature before slicing and serving.

Grapefruit's unusual, sharp flavour works brilliantly in baking, and takes the edge off the sweetness. Orange marmalade works well, too. The added moisture of the marmalade means that this cake takes longer to cook than most, but it's well worth the wait.

Serves 8–10

200g soft butter, plus extra
  for greasing

450g self-raising flour

2 tsp baking powder

350g light soft brown sugar

6 eggs

250g pink grapefruit or lemon and
  lime marmalade

75ml grapefruit juice, plus 3–4 tbsp

125ml milk

200g icing sugar

GRAPEFRUIT MARMALADE CAKE

Preheat the oven to 150°C/300°F/Gas mark 2. Grease and line a 24cm diameter springform cake tin with baking parchment. Put the flour, baking powder and butter in a bowl and rub together with your fingertips to form a breadcrumb-like consistency.

Stir in the sugar, then beat in the eggs, 75g of the marmalade, the 75ml grapefruit juice and the milk to form a thick batter. Pour the mixture into the cake tin and bake for 1 hour, until risen and golden. Check if the cake is cooked by inserting a clean skewer or knife into the centre – if it comes out clean, the cake is ready. If not, bake for a further 10 minutes and check once more. Allow to cool in the tin, then turn out onto a wire cooling rack.

Meanwhile, sift the icing sugar into a bowl and add 3–4 tbsp grapefruit juice, 1 tablespoon at a time, to make an icing the consistency of double cream. Slice the cake in half widthways and spread the bottom half with the remaining grapefruit marmalade. Place the other half on top of it, then spread the icing over the top and allow it to drizzle down the sides. Leave the icing to set before serving.

I have lots of figs growing in my garden — anyone with a south-facing garden can give fig growing a go. This can also be made in an ordinary cake tin, which will give you something more like an upside-down cake, but if you invest in a savarin mould it turns a cake into an easy dinner-party dessert.

Serves 8

250g strong white bread flour, plus
    extra for dusting

7g fast-action yeast

5g sea salt

320g caster sugar

115g beaten eggs (about
    3 medium eggs)

40ml milk

125g very soft butter, plus extra
    for greasing

4 figs

150ml fig liqueur

FIG SAVARIN

Put the flour, yeast, salt and 20g of the caster sugar in a stand mixer with a paddle attachment. Beat to combine, then add the beaten eggs and milk to form a soft dough. Beat for 5 minutes until smooth and elastic, then switch to the whisk attachment and gradually add the butter. Continue whisking until the butter is fully incorporated, then tip out onto a lightly floured work surface. Knead lightly to form a soft ball, then place in a large bowl, cover with clingfilm and set aside to prove for 1 hour.

Meanwhile, grease a 30cm fluted savarin tin and dust it with flour. Cut the figs in half lengthways and put them, cut-side down, into the prepared tin at regular intervals, pressing down gently.

Turn the dough out onto a floured surface and knead it lightly. Carefully place the dough into the savarin tin over the figs, pressing it down lightly to make sure it is even. Leave to prove for another hour until well risen.

Preheat the oven to 180°C/350°F/Gas mark 4. Put the savarin tin on a baking sheet and bake for 20 minutes. Reduce the temperature to 150°C/300°F/Gas mark 2 and bake for a further 40 minutes. Remove and allow to cool for 5 minutes before turning out onto a serving plate.

Meanwhile, put the remaining caster sugar, 150ml water and the fig liqueur in a pan and bring to the boil over a high heat. Cook for a few minutes until thickened and syrupy. Spoon the fig syrup over the savarin on the plate and baste it until all the syrup is used up. Serve at room temperature, cut into wedges.

This is a cross between a crumble and a cake, so you get the best of both worlds! It's simple to make, too, and a hit with kids. Pick the right time of year (late summer and early autumn), and blackberries are the best free foraged food you can get. There are lots of them near where I live, but you can use frozen ones instead – just make sure they are well dried before adding them to the mix.

Serves 8

CAKE:

250g butter, plus extra for greasing

250g light soft brown sugar

4 large eggs

250g self-raising flour

300g blackberries

CRUMBLE:

150g plain flour

75g butter, diced

75g demerara sugar

BLACKBERRY CRUMBLE CAKE

Preheat the oven to 170°C/325°F/Gas mark 3. Grease and line a 23cm diameter springform cake tin with baking parchment. Put the butter and sugar in a bowl and whisk until light and fluffy. Add the eggs, one at a time, beating well between each addition. Add the flour, fold it in, then spoon the mixture into the prepared tin. Scatter the blackberries over the top to cover completely.

To make the crumble, put the flour and butter in a bowl and rub the butter into the flour with your fingertips until the mix resembles fine breadcrumbs. Add the sugar and stir to combine. Sprinkle the crumble over the top of the blackberries.

Bake the cake in the oven for 60–80 minutes, until golden and cooked through. Check if the cake is cooked by inserting a clean skewer or knife into the centre – if it comes out clean, the cake is ready. If not, bake for a further 10 minutes and check once more. Remove from the oven and allow to cool in the tin before turning out.

I love collecting old recipe books – I've even got some from the early 1800s. This recipe comes from a book published at the start of the nineteenth century. Keiller's Bakery in Dundee is said to have started our love of this Scottish cake by mass-producing it. It's often served at Christmas and nearly always has almonds arranged on the top.

Serves 8–12

225g soft butter, plus extra
 for greasing

225g dark brown sugar

4 large eggs

grated zest of 1 unwaxed lemon

325g self-raising flour

15g ground mixed spice

50g ground almonds

100g sultanas

100g currants

50g chopped mixed peel

75g glacé cherries

125g raisins

150g whole blanched almonds

DUNDEE CAKE

Preheat the oven to 140°C/275°F/Gas mark 1. Grease and line the inside and outside of a 20cm diameter deep-sided cake tin with baking parchment.

Put the butter and sugar in a bowl and whisk until light and fluffy. Add the eggs one at a time, beating well after each addition, then fold in the lemon zest, flour, mixed spice and ground almonds, until well combined. Add all the mixed fruit and 50g of the almonds and stir again. Spoon into the prepared tin and level the top.

Decorate the top with the reserved whole almonds, then bake in the oven for 1¾ hours. Cover the top with baking parchment or foil halfway through if the top is browning too much. Check if the cake is cooked by inserting a clean skewer or knife into the centre – if it comes out clean, the cake is ready. If not, bake for a further 10 minutes and check once more. Remove and allow to cool in the tin for 15 minutes before turning out.

This is a great centrepiece for the kitchen table, and if your kitchen is anything like mine, the cake won't even have cooled down before it's all gone. Walnuts or macadamia nuts are also good in this, as are pears. Serve it with whipped double cream and some blueberry jam on the side.

Serves 8–10

100g caster sugar

50g walnut halves

100g soft butter, plus extra
    for greasing

340g plain flour, plus extra
    for dusting

2–3 Golden Delicious apples

250g caster sugar

2 eggs

1 tbsp baking powder

½ tsp salt

175ml double cream

100g blueberries

BLUEBERRY, APPLE AND WALNUT CAKE

Preheat the oven to 170°C/325°F/Gas mark 3. Put 100ml water and the sugar in a pan and bring to the boil. Simmer until the sugar has melted and the syrup has thickened a little. Add the walnuts and cook for 2–3 minutes. Drain the walnuts, discarding the syrup, place them on a sheet of baking parchment and allow to cool until just dry, then chop into 1cm pieces.

Grease and dust a 1kg loaf tin with flour, tapping out any excess. Slice the apples into thin circles and place in the tin, the edges just touching, to cover the bottom, sides and ends of the tin.

Put the butter and sugar in a bowl and whisk until light and fluffy. Beat in the eggs one at a time, beating well after each addition. Sift the flour, baking powder and salt together, then add, a little at a time, to the butter and egg mixture. Fold in alternately with the double cream until everything is just combined. Fold in the blueberries and walnuts.

Carefully pour the mixture into the prepared tin, taking care to keep the apples in place on the sides. Bake in the oven for 1 hour 20 minutes, until just cooked. Check if the cake is cooked by inserting a clean skewer or knife into the centre – if it comes out clean, the cake is ready. If not, bake for a further 10 minutes and check once more. Allow to cool in the tin for 10 minutes before turning out to cool completely.

This is a traditional method for making a cake, but the basil isn't a traditional addition. Using it in cakes and puddings gives them the flavour of pistachios – it sounds odd, but it really does. It's great with lemon, and next time you have strawberries, try them with fresh basil. It was one of my chef's ideas to blend the sugar with the basil for the topping, and it works a treat.

Serves 10

100g melted butter, plus extra
  for greasing
250g plain flour, plus extra
  for dusting
grated zest and juice of
  4 unwaxed lemons

350g caster sugar
6 eggs
150ml double cream
pinch of salt
½ tsp baking powder
25g fresh basil

LEMON AND BASIL CAKE

Preheat the oven to 170°C/325°F/Gas mark 3. Grease and dust a 1kg loaf tin with flour, tapping out any excess.

Put the lemon zest in a large mixing bowl with 300g of the sugar, eggs, cream, salt and melted butter. Whisk with an electric hand whisk until light and fluffy, then gradually add the flour and baking powder. Pour the mixture into the prepared tin and bake in the oven for 1 hour.

Check if the cake is cooked by inserting a clean skewer or knife into the centre – if it comes out clean, the cake is ready. If not, bake for a further 10 minutes and check once more.

Meanwhile, strain the lemon juice into a small food processor and add the remaining 50g sugar and basil leaves and stalks. Process to a fine purée, then pass through a sieve into a bowl.

Spoon the basil syrup over the cake and leave it to soak in for 30 minutes, until all the liquid has been absorbed. Remove from the tin, slice and serve warm or cold.

When we were testing the recipes for this book, this is the one that got eaten the most quickly. Glacé cherries aren't an ingredient chefs use very much, but they're brilliant in this cake. You can't make it with fresh cherries, as they sink and they're too moist.

Serves 8

230g soft butter, plus extra
    for greasing

230g plain flour, plus extra
    for dusting

80g dried cherries

80g sour cherries

90g glacé cherries

1 vanilla pod

230g caster sugar, plus 2 tbsp

4 large eggs

100g ground almonds

½ tsp baking powder

2 tbsp milk

THREE-CHERRY CAKE

Preheat the oven to 180°C/350°F/Gas mark 4 and lightly grease a 20cm diameter, 10cm deep cake tin. Dust it with a little flour, then line the base with baking parchment. Put the dried and sour cherries into a bowl and cover with boiling water. Leave to soak for 15 minutes, then drain the cherries, discarding the water. Pat the cherries dry and toss with 2 tbsp of the flour. Cut the glacé cherries in half.

Split the vanilla pod in half lengthways and scrape out the seeds. Put the butter, vanilla seeds and sugar in a mixing bowl and whisk with an electric hand whisk until light in colour. This should take about 5 minutes. Add the eggs, one at a time, whisking continuously – this will prevent the mixture from splitting.

Fold in the cherries and ground almonds, then sift in the flour and baking powder and fold in well. Add the milk and carefully but quickly mix all the ingredients together. Pour into the prepared tin. Level the top with the spoon and bake on the middle shelf of the oven for 1 hour. Cover it with foil and bake for a further 10 minutes.

Check if the cake is cooked by inserting a clean skewer or knife into the centre – if it comes out clean, the cake is ready. If not, bake for a further 10 minutes and check once more. Once cooked, remove from the oven, sprinkle with the reserved caster sugar and allow to cool in the tin for 15 minutes before turning out. Slice and serve – it's great with lightly whipped double cream.

index